Simon O'Toole

CONFESSIONS OF AN AMERICAN SCHOLAR

UNIVERSITY OF MINNESOTA PRESS · MINNEAPOLIS

ISBN-0-8166-0583-1.

Published in Great Britain, India, and Pakistan by the Oxford University Press, London, Bombay, and Karachi, and in Canada by the Copp Clark Publishing Co. Limited, Toronto.

Professor O'Toole is a well-known scholar in his field, which he has described to us as a small pasture about eight feet by twelve. He has taught at black and white colleges, private and public colleges, Ivy League and brick colleges, bad and worse colleges, and he liked the black worst one best, though he was fired from it after a year. The number of his publications over the past decade has made many of his colleagues nervous. He says that this cautionary tale concerns only the literary scholar. Of the gay, useful, rewarding, and Knowledgeable lives of American historians, academic scientists, philosophers, and sociologists, he insists he knows nothing, except what is recorded in chapters 12 and 13.

TABLE OF CONTENTS

Confessions of an
American Scholar

1

WIDE-EYED YOUNGSTER AND CROSS-EYED KNOWLEDGE

I suppose you would have to call me a triumphant product of American education. Thirty years ago I was a poor and happy boy in a small town where almost no one went to college, and I won a scholarship to a great university, and here I am today, stoop-shouldered and weary, with the nasty burden of Wisdom on my back. How did I let it happen to me, and who is to blame besides myself? I will tell you my story not because it is unusual but because it is typical.

I go back to that glorious spring morning when my life was changed. I was playing baseball at recess in high school, and the secretary of the principal came out to say that I was wanted, and I trotted inside in my shorts and T-shirt, hoping that my girl friend would see me as I passed her classroom. The principal was a beady-eyed man who didn't like me. I had once written an impolite letter to a debating coach at another school who turned out to be a friend of his. When I needed the principal's recommendation to apply for my scholarship, I went and apologized to him, and he knew how much of my heart was in it. But this morning he had a letter in his hand saying I had won a full-tuition scholarship ($450 in those days) to my great university. He was sober rather than ecstatic, and he urged me to be sober too; but I rushed outside and looked at the blue sky and thought of the wonder of the universe.

"What did they want, Simon?"

"I won a scholarship to X."

"Gee."

At noon I rushed home to my mother, whose pride I was, and she told me it was the happiest day of her life.

I was not the cleverest boy in the world. My I.Q. came to 122 or 128, I forget which, and though I was the highest ranking boy in my class, I had little taste for study. I was an outdoor boy, with love for the smells of the earth and for the exercise of my body. I did my schoolwork with my left hand, and the admissions people at X thought I would do C plus work for them. My scholarship required altruism and influence. X University was just then embarking on its program to find hidden talent, and a cardinal rule of such programs is that I.Q. and aptitude tests and grades and recommendations are sometimes wrong. There is the x-factor, and somebody thought I had it. That somebody was an alumnus of X, whom my father knew. This man was a rich man, and my father was a poor man, but they were both chicken fanciers, and my father was the better man there. My father told his friend about me, and one day I made a trip to see the man, and all I remember is that he asked me whether I could play the piano, and I said no; but I was a poetical-looking boy, and that must have counted.

So a trap was laid for me, but I walked into it gladly. My mother had seen to that. She knew it would be fine for me to be a scientist with a Ph.D., and she used to tell me about the great man she had known when she was a child, who was a biologist at Columbia University and who was privileged to take her on walks into forbidden areas of New York's Botanical Gardens. I built myself a laboratory in our backyard, and much enjoyed the building of it, but I was no more a budding scientist than I was a fish, and was no more a budding anything else either. Still I had to think about the future, or rather I was told to think about the future; and

[4

my school helped my mother in prodding me along. Everyone assumed I was going to college, and I was given catalogues from Columbia, Harvard, Princeton, and Chicago to pore over. They were magical things, those catalogues, full of mysteries beyond the mysteries of encyclopedias. Merely to read a description of an exotic course was for me to see a temple of learning crowded with bearded men from the corners of the earth. I had no connection with these men, I didn't see myself joining them. If I had a dream at all, it was to run faster than Glenn Cunningham. But the catalogues were a great romance, and I liked the smell and size and form of the Columbia one best. I can't remember why I didn't apply there.

In due time I arrived at X, and I continued to be led along a path marvelous and strange. Of the temple itself — Collegiate Gothic and Instant Georgian — some people had made mockery, and I was there only a short time before I learned about the fakery of it all. But I was not bothered. Recently I took a young girl around the place, and it was not the fakery but the ugliness of the stone and the monotony of the decoration that I told her about. And she said: "Still it's the most beautiful thing I've ever seen." That was the way I felt. I felt that way about the whole institution. In my freshman English course we read *The Ordeal of Richard Feverel*, and had regular ten-minute quizzes on it that were a mystery to me. I never had a clue to what the next one would be about. They shattered me, made a fool of me, and the novel became confused in my mind with the ordeal of Simon O'Toole. But I didn't blame the instructor. I thought he was handing down mysteries from on high. In years since, I have learned how to give clever quizzes myself, and I know that any fool can do it; but then I knew nothing.

I did most of my learning outside class. I didn't dislike my classes, but never went to any of them with genuine longing. The real moments were the stolen ones, times when I should have been reading physics or Kant but shut my mind against them and curled up with *Of Time and the River, Sons and Lovers, Thurso's Landing.* Or went down to the local record shop and ran through Mozart's last symphonies in four hours, comparing Toscanini and Beecham and getting my Köchel numbers straight as well as the AM, DM, MM label numbers of Victor and Columbia — all of it attracting so much more energy than anything a classroom could compel.

But I did have one good moment in class, and I have always thought of it as the most important moment in my life. That it was an accident, that it would have occurred somehow or other in college or out, hardly detracts from my gratitude. When I was in high school, my mother gave me a copy of *Childe Harold's Pilgrimage*. She recommended its wisdom, and I found it much to my liking. I never vexed with mirth the drowsy ear of night, but the passions, renunciations, miseries, and profundities of Childe Harold shook me to my depths. When I went to college I found myself surrounded by boys whose I.Q.'s were 150 and who talked easily about the politics of Theodore Roosevelt; but I could always say under my breath: I bet you don't know *Childe Harold's Pilgrimage* by heart. It was the cornerstone of my adolescence, and the mark of my mother upon my soul. Came the day when I studied Byron in one of my classes, and my much admired professor ridiculed *Childe Harold* and said that the real Byron was in *Don Juan*. This was a cataclysm. How could my mother be wrong? How could I be wrong? How could my professor be wrong? I began to grow up that day.

But on the whole my classes and the entire program of work at X University seemed to have little bearing on what I was or what I wanted. I accepted it all as God-given, and maintained a kind of reverence for the place, and yet it was something out there, something I had to put up with, a vast maze that I was wandering through. I would infallibly come out at the end, but to what end? I had energy and quickness of mind; I wanted joy and perception; and people kept telling me to sit in a classroom.

There is nothing strange in all this. It must have been the commonest experience of college boys of my generation. The world was not the world we made but the world we were driven into. It was there, hard, dull, and real, and who were we to imagine it could be otherwise? I can't blame myself that I went through college thinking that my vague discontent was my own fault instead of the fault of the wise men about me. What is strange is that I left that life and came back to it a few years later as a teacher, and saw that my task was to give clever quizzes, to cajole and otherwise to drive my wide-eyed youngsters along the path to Knowledge. Things are different today, but not different enough.

My experience at X was epitomized in an extreme way by a single nasty moment I had there. I used to do odd jobs to earn pocket money, and occasionally the psychology department had me in for experiments in memory process. They gave me a half-dozen pairs of nonsense syllables, and my task was to learn to name the second of each pair as the first was flashed at me. One day I was introduced to what was described as a refined version of the same thing, and some sort of sensing device was put on my head and wrists. Then the experimenter said: "Do you masturbate?" That poor man does not know for how long afterward he was hated and despised. I gave him my "No," and his sensors recorded the leap of shame in my heart, and he had his knowledge, and we went on to our nonsense. And that is why I hated him: I was his victim, and so innocent a victim that I hardly thought he was doing wrong. He was a seeker after Truth and I lied to him. I was unworthy to begin with, and he learned my unworthiness. Twenty years later I sat in a garden one morning and read that the psychology department at X was conducting experiments in how people react to scenes of torture. Same old university, I said to myself; same old torturers.

My career at X ended not quite in a blaze of glory. I began in physics because my mother wanted me to, and I wound up in English because I wanted to. My grades all round were spotty, but in English I had A's and B's, and on a few papers I had A pluses. The x-factor was that I had memorized *Childe Harold*, the *Rubáiyát*, the sonnets of Elizabeth Barrett Browning, Shakespeare, and Edna St. Vincent Millay. I wasn't clever about literature, I merely loved it, bits and pieces of it, and my love carried me most of the way. On a signal occasion, though, it failed, and I hardly knew why. The university sponsored a prize essay contest for seniors in English — seventy-five pages of original writing, to be weighed by a committee of august professors. I wrote on Hart Crane. In those years

Crane was an underground figure, whom one heard of by word of mouth from the most poetical of one's friends. The day I obtained his *Collected Poems* from the library was a rare day in my life. Here was a building with four million books in it, and I wanted a volume that was known to almost no one. The book itself when it came was a marvelous thing, with its odd format, the large almost square shape, the fine dull red cover, the imprint of an unknown publisher, the marginal glosses. I could hardly help giving to Hart Crane all the fierce devotion of a secret passion. The recondite essay by Waldo Frank, included in the book, gave fuel to the passion, as also did the biography by Philip Horton I got hold of. This happened a year or more before the contest. When I came to write my essay I was able to find little else written on Crane.

My way with essays before then was pure enthusiasm and emotion. I loved Amelia and suffered with Dobbin throughout *Vanity Fair*, and when I read the words "grow green again, tender little violet" my heart fairly burst with anguished joy, and I could translate it all in a flood of my own prose. But twenty pages in a large hand was some distance from seventy-five of typing, and my enthusiasm for Crane carried me a very few steps before I saw the trouble I was in. I could recite half of *The Bridge* by heart, and I could tell you that Crane was Walt Whitman's heir and twice as modern as T. S. Eliot, but after that I was stuck, and had to go back to Waldo Frank and Philip Horton. I don't know whether I actually plagiarized these men, but it was clear to me that my paper was their paper. None of us won the prize.

I was baffled and dispirited by this experience. Luckily I did not know that my future lay in being able to say clever and original things about novels and poetry. Waldo Frank was no scholar, and now that Crane has become an important figure, scholars write immensely clever and unreadable books on him. Yet in my bafflement I had a glimmering of what I seem to have learned in the course of another twenty-five years — that there is knowledge which is love, joy, and perception, and there is Knowledge, which is dry, ugly, and sterile. I have served Knowledge most of my adult life, along with my colleagues. We bear the marks of our trade.

I left X after my seventh term to go to war, and was granted my degree in absentia. The university allowed one's military experience to count as a semester of education. In my absence I began to learn about irreverence.

2

GRADUATE SCHOOL; OR, WHAT'S A NICE BOY LIKE
YOU DOING IN A PLACE LIKE THIS?

Somewhere there must be an American scholar who actually wanted
to be an American scholar. I have never met him. What I mean is that I
have never had the effrontery to say to one of my colleagues: Was it this
that you dreamed of in your bright college years? Did you have a genuine
adolescent longing to write footnotes, to write books that would turn your
face ashen and humorless? No, I have a hard time believing such a person
exists. The end product exists, but the end product is a mistaken calculation. The adolescent begins by liking literature, by thinking he will write
novels and poetry, by lacking an appetite for science, by having an urge
to make the world better, by needing to escape the draft, by wanting to
avoid work. Graduate school happens to him; then teaching; then scholarship. I do know men who may have been born to be American scholars,
but I have to guess. One of them was with me at Brunch University, a
fellow instructor ten years my junior and much more likely to succeed, a
man with a card index for a mind and with a devotion to scholarship — or
to getting ahead in scholarship — that made him a wonder to everyone
but his wife. He was a dreadful teacher and his students rose up against

him, but that is another story and did not affect his career in the least. One day at my house he referred casually to his current work as "the book of my young manhood." I knew then that I was talking to a man from Mars. My god I wanted to publish a book, but "a book of my young manhood"? I never dreamed in such terms. That bright young man got his promotion a year before I was even considered, though we arrived at Brunch the same year. And in another year he was off to a better paying job, and in two more years had moved up to a more prestigious university than Brunch. And I put myself on Mars momentarily and realized that he must be possessed of a dream unmentionable — to get to Harvard by the age of thirty-two. And the curious thing is that although he has published articles in the best places, read papers at meetings of the Modern Language Association, and even edited a classic British novel, he has not yet published the book of his young manhood or reached Harvard. Ten years gone now. I knew another man who shocked me in the same way by telling me when we were both twenty-eight years old and instructors at a small college that he had promised himself to be a full professor before he was forty. Imagine that! But he was in languages, not literature.

For myself, graduate school and the scholarly life were something that I walked into backwards. I came out of the army in 1946 full of weltschmerz that the Germans had helped give to me, and I wanted (not very badly) to write a great novel to display my tears to the world. For several months I drew an unemployment check and read Kierkegaard and Freud and thought about the future. So far as I knew I had four choices, all unlikely, open to me: journalism, editorial-publishing work, teaching, and graduate school. The last, courtesy of an altruistic government, was merely a dim horror. I had no intention of sitting in a classroom again, and the day I actually did start my first graduate course was a gray day of admitted failure. Journalism I felt I had no talent for. Of editorial-publishing work I knew nothing. Teaching was it — not public school teaching but private, or perhaps lower grade college. So I wound up at a kind of junior college earning $2,000 a year, teaching fifteen hours a week, and spending another fifty hours preparing my classes, reading papers, and talking with students. My novel lay untouched, and after several months I realized that what I needed was a job of purely manual labor that would leave me free after eight hours a day and leave my mind free even during those eight hours. I quit at the end of the year and got my laboring job, and found that it exhausted me physically and left my mind numb. I also fell in love and had to save my girl from an unhappy home. There I was, all of a sudden, married and still wanting to write my novel. What was I to do but accept the gratitude of my country and take life easy as a student once again? And so I did. When I received my Ph.D., a mere ten years later, my university — Orlon University, let me call it — waived the writing of eight term papers that I had not attended to. I had written two novels instead, both of them so bad that it fills me full of the tears of things to recall them.

Now Orlon University was one of the well-known universities, not the supposed best in the land, but if anyone were asked to name the twenty best, it would surely be found somewhere on the list between ten and twenty. When I was there, it was considered somewhat behind the times, but having had experience of the very best and very worst, before and since, I am sure that the same characters lurk everywhere. Most of the men at Yale are fit to teach at Bob Jones University, and the men at Bob Jones are doubtless fit to teach at Bob Jones. At any rate I went with due reluctance into that first graduate course and had one of the surprises of my life. The course was in Restoration literature, and it was presided over by a lump of dough whom I might as well call Lump. Lump had a method to the classroom sessions, namely to save himself work, and so he gave us a problem to solve: what is the meaning of the word "neoclassic"? Each student had an author to prepare and read a paper on, to see whether or not the author's works fitted into the several definitions of neoclassic that we were offered for a start. With thirty students in the course, and the course meeting once a week, Lump got away with lecturing to us only two or three times. For the most part he sat in the front row taking notes on what each student said as though he were a student himself. So we went our turns, the real victims sitting in mournful silence while the lucky one or two got some exercise. At the end of each exercise, Lump rose and said a few irrelevant words, and that was that. By the time my turn came around, I was furious. If I was nothing else, I was not a lump of dough, and the fraud being perpetrated upon us was not going to be given a polite assent in my paper. So on my day I argued, with some passion and with George Farquhar as my text, that the enterprise we were embarked on was absurd. I did this with fear in my heart, I may say, for Lump did certainly know more about the subject than I knew, and with a few questions afterward he could make a fool of me. I sat down breathless and flushed. Lump said: "Very interesting, Mr. O'Toole; the most interesting paper we've had. So you think we are not likely to arrive at a definition of neoclassic?" That was all. I realized that I had cowed the man. Strange experience! Class was over, and two students stopped by my desk and shook my hand.

I got an A in that course, though aside from the paper I did very little work; and the A was based solely on the paper. For when the final examination came, the only other basis for a grade, I was caught squarely on a topic about which I knew almost nothing, and it was the only topic. I gassed for two hours, and went home knowing that it was all up with graduate school. Lump would be glad to pay me back for my earlier impertinence. But he must have saved himself still more work and not read the examination papers. So I had an A for my Farquhar paper. What a tribute to Lump's scholarly objectivity! Surely it *was* the best paper read in that class; and a year later I used it, with suitable alterations, in another course. And that A, along with reasonable grades in my other first-term courses, launched me upon my career.

Most of my other courses weren't as bad as Lump's. Some of them were worse. Oh the prize course in that direction, will I ever forget it? The man who conducted it deserved a name like Lumpenlumpen Galumph, but for a reason that will emerge in a moment I will call him Puck. He had much less to say than Lump, but made a greater effort to say it, and he talked with a stammer — it seemed deliberately — to protract our agony. What he did was to recite bibliography at us, hour by hour, spelling out words and names we knew, and he took attendance so that we had to endure it most of the time. I used to sit there saying to myself, "I am going to die," "I am dead," and writing obscene limericks upon his name. And this man was a well-known scholar, authority on a serenely civilized novelist.

It won't do, and it wouldn't be fair, to continue with a catalogue of the morose, dull, and empty-headed men who cut Spenser, Pope, Coleridge, and many others down to their own size. How does it happen that a man spends his life in the company of Shakespeare and shows no sign even of a sense of humor, let alone some small flight of imagination? Mystery of American scholarship! Let me instead praise three men I had, and if the praise is still barbed, that must be taken as the reservation of a person who thought, and still thinks, that the scholarly profession can have something high if not mighty about it. The least of the three first. He was a man with a large idea—namely organicism; and he had written what was taken to be a seminal article on the subject. Other people made careers out of applying this man's idea to Mark Twain, Emily Dickinson, and Evelyn Waugh; such was the glory of the idea, it could be applied everywhere; and I remember the start I had in this man's course on nineteenth-century English prose when he rang in Beethoven and Martha Graham to elucidate the organicism of Thomas Carlyle's work. Still it's something to be startled. The unpleasant part of the man's idea was that it gave chronology undue importance. If Carlyle's thought was organic, we could see the organ only by knowing the exact sequence of his writing. Much tedium. But the man had something to talk about, and his enthusiasm, grasp, and ingenuity interested us. God knows what has happened to him in the nineteen years since I took his course. If that was his only idea, I would hate to see him again.

The next man was of a sort that they don't make nowadays, the last of a line of German-trained American scholars whose approach to literature was largely philological. I am sure that most of the ills of modern American scholarship trace in large part to the German tradition, but also there is a great gulf between the bristling scholar of today, armed with American weapons, and his old-fashioned predecessor. And it doesn't surprise me how much more I am inclined to like the predecessor than his heir, and I think the reason may be that his interests were so peripheral to literature that he saved some grace in his attention to it — whereas the modern scholar is all for searching out the heart of Hamlet's mystery, and goes at it with knife and club. This old man — he was past normal retirement age — was the easy master of a dozen languages — Old High German, Old High French, Old English, and all the ups and downs thereafter, along with Latin and Greek and maybe a few others. He more or less read his lectures to us — not lectures composed forty years before but lectures still in the process of composition, with the latest evidence on Chaucer's date of birth fitted into the whole argument on that subject. And that sort of thing was his concern — dates, the five meanings of a particular Chaucer word, the number of pilgrims who went on Chaucer's pilgrimage. Every now and then he would make a polite allusion to one of the more absurd misunderstandings of Chaucer's vocabulary made by the New Critics (then middle-aged). But what I chiefly remember was the sweetness and pedantic gaiety of the man. He loved Chaucer, and loved him for reasons that he did not talk about but that came across to us. A successful scholar, and the more I think of it, the more it seems that the likes of him might reasonably have dreamed in their youth of the pleasures of writing footnotes. Fifty years at his task had not withered him; and though it was he who assigned me those eight papers that I never wrote — examining the contents of a monastic library, such things as that — I have always thought of him with affection and gratitude. I cut his classes outrageously.

The third man was a man in motion. He trotted. When he sat still, he trotted. The engine was always going. The least interesting of his lectures was a tour de force of rhetoric, in which he constructed huge periodic sentences that floated to us like fugal music. At his best that music was hard with fact, energy, and imagination. He was the one man I felt I learned something from, and what I learned was not fact — though he was trained in the old school and was concerned to know when Philip

15]

Massinger was born — but I learned the passion, brilliance, grotesquerie of some of the sixteenth- and seventeenth-century dramatists whom he lived among. Their fire burned in him, and I saw their fire through him. Yet he was his own self, a square-faced, heavyset Michigan backwoodsman, aloof, unfriendly, and fearful to meet. Not a man I wanted to emulate. He was reported never to give more than a B on term papers, so severe were his standards, so critical his mentality; and the A minuses I got from him were the prizes of all my papers.

But what lean fare the whole show was! Never once did I say to myself that this was a world I wanted to belong to. And how strange that is: the few students I ever talked to were as appalled as I by the place, and most of them presently got jobs at obscure colleges, and to a man they would have given their right arm to be invited back to teach in the windy halls they hated. Myself included. The reason was prestige. We knew that if we taught at Orlon University we could at least look every other American scholar in the eye. Several years later when I was attending a meeting of the Modern Language Association, I visited the hotel room of a friend of mine who was teaching at one of the most prestigious of eastern universities. On my lapel was the sad legend: Simon O'Toole, Baraboo University. Two colleagues of his entered the room, and he introduced me. They looked not at me but at that legend, and did I see a look of disdain cross their faces? No — disdain is not quite the word. It was the glance of book reviewers who can tell by the opening paragraph that they will dismiss a particular book in a phrase. No matter what the book thinks of them! So my friend's colleagues read me in reading my lapel. So I hated to be read.

But that was in the pleasant future, and now I was accumulating points for my degree, along with other part-time or full-time students: nuns and priests who turned up in courses where G. M. Hopkins was studied, public school teachers getting credits for pay raises, a few old maids, a few young maids (whatever do *they* think they get out of it?), and fellow ex-soldiers. We traveled into the large city where Orlon University stood, once, twice, or three times a week, sat in our two-hour

[16

classes, and disappeared again. After a year or half a dozen years of such epiphanies we found ourselves with masters' degrees, and after another timeless interval some of us completed our coursework for the Ph.D. Surely one of the presidents of Orlon has described his realm as a great throbbing heart, pumping intellectual juices into students, who are the arteries, veins, and capillaries that spread out across a large state. But no, it's not like that. It's not even like an octopus and its tentacles.

3

GETTING MY DISSERTATION DONE BEFORE
MY HAIR FELL OUT

My friends have told me about their dissertations — great lumps of concrete that they had to shove three hundred miles along a straight and narrow path, and sometimes failed even to nudge. Poor lads! I myself wrote two dissertations, and the second provided the one moment of great triumph and discovery in my scholarly career. That the discovery was a piece of nonsense was neither here nor there.

I rather looked forward to doing a dissertation. Perhaps I would write on Hart Crane, who didn't exist so far as my teachers knew, and I would prove that his poetics equaled Milton's — something to let them know they were dead, most of them. But there was no twentieth-century scholar at Orlon University with whom I could write such a dissertation. Eventually I persuaded my Michigan backwoodsman to supervise "A Critical Analysis of Modern English Tragedy." That was grander than Hart Crane.

I had a free year in which to do the work. My wife and I went to live on baked beans in a village twenty miles from the university, and I was soon accumulating notes as though I were breeding rabbits. I had read a bit of modern American tragedy, not much English. Before I read any more, I needed to have criteria, and where would I get them except in theories of tragedy? I read theories of tragedy, but what was theory except an edifice built upon historical origins? I studied the origins of tragedy, and what were they but traces in the passage of a state of mind that goat-danced and sang before tearing its eyes out? Some anthropology was called for, most especially psychoanalytical anthropology. Do you know Géza Róheim? I knew him. And presently I knew that what I needed was a theory of one corner of the human mind, namely a theory of art; and if a theory of art required an understanding of the whole of the human mind — to say nothing of egg tempera, fan vaulting, and stage lighting — I would go after it. At the end of my year, I had a bibliography of several hundred items, the most eclectic bibliography ever assembled, and I had one hundred and fifty pages of dissertation on materials of art — all the arts. I sent this off to my adviser and asked him if he thought the English department would settle for a theory of art, which I could complete in another eight hundred pages.

It was mad only north northwest. Swear in your heart that you do not believe in cause and effect, evolution, sciences of mind and reality. Swear that you are not a mechanist who imagines that anything can be explained if enough or all of the facts are known. Scientists are reported to deplore Einstein's having spent his later years in search of a unified field theory, but I dare say he was no more absurd then than when he invented the theory of relativity. Ernest Jones tells of how Freud was preoccupied by a universal theory of numbers a short while before he began to study his dreams, and if this proves to you how far genius can travel in a little space, then all the swearing in your heart will not convince me you are not a mechanist. I was a mechanist. I thought things could be explained once and for all, and I was so little willing to get merely a short distance from Truth that I tried to swallow the universe whole. That dissertation had to be abandoned, and in years afterward I reproached my adviser for letting me get started on the original immodest topic. But now I see that I had to do it. I was stupid, and had to learn what I know the hard way. What I know is what William Blake knew when he described science as Newton's sleep. Say Darwin's sleep too, and Einstein's, and Freud's — the sleep of people at the foot of the tree of Knowledge. And say that the American scholar sleeps most unsoundly of all, and dreams that he shares the company of great men.

Eventually I went back to Orlon to get a new topic. And after more trouble I found myself saying to a new adviser: you name the topic, and I will do it. I was not going to fail again, I was going to take a dull absurd topic and play the game out. We settled the thing with some concession to my interests. Ian McPherson (1875–1945), Irish-born poet and man of letters, was next to last in my choice of six possible authors to work on, and the subject itself was my last choice — Images of Disease in the Poems of. My wife and I bought some more beans, and I started a new pursuit after this smaller universe.

For you do not suppose that I had my lesson perfect yet. I swallowed McPherson whole. Now McPherson was not an easy man to swallow. He was a prodigious poet, one of those men you stumble across in the British Museum catalogue — you may never have heard of them but there they are with two hundred titles to their names. I got hold of all his books, all the books on him, dissertations written in France and Germany, articles and squibs by the hundreds. I wrote to T. S. Eliot and Ralph Hodgson to get their opinions on fine points. I did it all in several gulps, while my adviser stood by startled and acquiescent. In the end I handed him six hundred pages of a critical study in which images of disease figured in fifty. That man has my deepest gratitude. He knew I had to do it, and he knew I could do it, and once I was on my way, rushing past images of disease like a hot meteor, he bade me godspeed.

But Ian McPherson — do you know his dull, pedestrian, absolutely unimaginative verse that goes by the name of poetry? A poet meant to be swallowed whole, not chewed and digested, a poet fit for students to write dissertations about. So I thought, and I read through his seven epics, fifty-eight romances, and forty-three volumes of lyric poetry and essays, and thought the same, and most of his critics thought the same, and then I started through his works again. I knew that I could not judge his first poem until I read his last, or his last until I judged the first in light of the last. Such was my right-mindedness, such my energy, and they had their reward, for in the middle of the second reading I had an apocalyptic vision. I was reading one of his narrative poems about low life, a tale about a mad chimney sweep, and I chanced to meditate upon the fact that the action takes place in Tower Hamlets, London. Why should McPherson have chosen Tower Hamlets? The mad chimney sweep has a wicked uncle, a disreputable mother, and a faithless fiancée. Could it be? Yes it could be. My dull poem about low life was an extraordinary retelling of the Hamlet legend, and all the critics who had ever written on McPherson were blind.

You who have been fed on archetypes and allegories are unimpressed. Not long ago I glanced at a novel by a popular novelist who holds a high post at a famous university, and I saw that the daredevil hero's name was Fust and his girl's name was Margaret, and I groaned to think of the day when some dissertation student would realize he was in the presence of the Faust legend. But my perception about McPherson was not academic. It was of a kind that is possible to men who swallow their universes whole, who are living deeply and completely in a subject, whose minds are freighted with a million unsorted facts, facts that are not facts but pieces of meaninglessness. Suddenly there is crystallization, the sands turn to diamonds, the fire of work becomes the dance of knowledge. For several days I lived in a euphoria of perception, in which scene after scene in all McPherson's poems cascaded before me in Shakespearean dress. And this knowledge came without meaning: it presented itself, and left me to wonder why it should be and what it implied. But I was content to let it happen. And so pure and complete was the experience that I felt my whole life was transformed. I was on the other side of a great divide, and my life must somehow be richer. I told myself this was nonsense, the euphoria would pass, and I would be my old unpleasant self. But I did revere that experience, and the memory of it touches me even now.

After several days I had to become a scholar again, and settle down to comparing McPherson line by line with Shakespeare. It was harder than I thought. Most of the action of the chimney-sweep tale takes place in a pub called "The Denmark," run by the uncle. Well and good. But can a pub be compared with Claudius's court? Consider that the uncle sees himself "holding court" there. Consider that he plays the clarinet, also drums, and drinks to excess ("And as he drains his draughts of Rhenish down,/The kettledrum and trumpet thus bray out"). Consider that the pub is haunted and that the sweep and his friend 'orace see a ghost there. Unconvincing? I could — and did — add two dozen other details to make the comparison stick. Then I showed that the attic where the sweep keeps some books is Wittenberg. Somewhat less convincing, even to me. It became a morass that I waded around in, always exhilarated and always troubled. Was I to assume that every last scene and word in the poem bore a deliberate Shakespearean reference? Or did McPherson lay on the comparison lightly, or even accidentally, or even unconsciously? I opted for every last scene and word, and thought I was going to prove that McPherson and I were as clever as James Joyce — especially in the images of the poor hero sweeping to his revenge. I did so in seventy pages that stand in unsullied splendor only in the first draft of the dissertation. Every time I revised the dissertation in the next few years I pared those pages down, removing my wildest leaps, until finally in my published book the subject is treated almost as a joke that McPherson enjoyed with himself, a private entertainment to relieve the tedium of writing verse, a pattern whose threads and ends only he himself could properly pick out again.

One learns, doesn't one. The paring of those pages was undertaken in part because my adviser and others read them in disbelief. It wasn't till long past the final paring that I had my lesson perfect, and knew that the general strategy of scholarly investigation in America — whether enlightened by occasional visions or merely conducted with shovel and fine-tooth comb — leads to ignorance. That is a broad unscholarly statement, to be sure, and what else should it be? Should I prove that American scholarship is absurd by conducting a scholarly investigation? I have already done that. But say that I was unlucky with the Shakespearean allusions in McPherson: am I willing to condemn every piece of sound scholarship I have produced since then, and am I willing to condemn all the wisdom that graces all the best books and articles I have ever read in American journals?

The scientist tells us that the brick we see — so hard and sharp and heavy — is in motion, is in the air and of the air, is transparent, quivering. So it is to men of single vision, who have narrowed their normal eyesight to an extreme mechanical perception. This is the glory of science, this simple-mindedness, that enables men in Los Angeles and Bombay to see things the same way, and would enable Newton to see things Einstein's way if only he could be restored to his scientific senses. And this glory is several cuts above the glory that enables you and me to see the hard brick, for in a moment we may be quarreling about whether it is a handsome brick. The scholar, luckless man, is confronted with a poem, so much less substantial than a brick that he never knows where the surface is; but he is not bothered; he thinks the poem is a scientific brick that he can dive into and come through covered in glory. Watch him carve up and parcel out the images. Watch him, as Freud's heir apparent, analyze the characters in the poem, the character of the author in the poem, the poem as character. Watch him roll the seventeenth century into a ball and throw it at the poem. We know the absurd results. That man who spent several years writing sixty-page analyses of Keats's odes — is he not a serious and devoted man, and can you rise from reading those analyses and swear you have not traveled three thousand miles in the wrong direction? That man who gave forty years to accumulating all the truest facts of the life of you-know-who — has he not buried his poor author in a definitive grave? You name the literary strategy that makes sense to you, and there are armies of scholars against you, men whose single vision is not your single vision. Luckless profession, where we all try hard to be right, and are all dead wrong. Sometimes this predicament breeds modesty, and the scholar sees himself not so much a wise man as a humble worker helping to build the great dome of Knowledge and realizing he may be doing a bad job. Recently I read a review of a new book on

Spenser. This book, said the reviewer, would have been a good book fifteen years ago, but the present state of Spenser scholarship calls for this, this, and this to be done, and the author says nothing about them. The reviewer made me see how well the building of the Spenser dome was going forward, with the reviewer himself as temporary supervisor, trying to eliminate laziness and incompetence. In due time, I could be sure, the job would be done, and there would be Spenser bricked up inside. Have you read the recent best Spenser scholarship?

I know another modest man, a man with a photographic mind, who told me one day that he had been invited to edit *Hamlet* for a Canadian publisher. He was not happy. In twenty-five years, he said, all the textual problems of that play would be solved, and a definitive edition could be produced. But anything he did now would be imperfect and ephemeral. You get the character of his modesty. This man, I may say, was a standing wonder to me. How could he know so much and know so little? He was able to recite Shakespeare's plays backwards without undue trouble, and he knew the criticism of two centuries inside out, and yet he could not tell a good performance from a bad performance of one of the plays. Recall the simple-minded explanations of Hamlet's problem that Goethe and his fellows entertained, and imagine my photographer full of the latest most subtle wisdom of all sorts — a multiple-visioned scholar if you like. Will you believe that Goethe understood Hamlet less perfectly than my photographer? I did not. In time the wonder of him ceased, and I came to think that he was standing proof that American scholarship produces ignorance. He thought he kept the company of Shakespeare, but really he kept the company of the computer that was solving his textual problems. He wanted to be dragged into eternity on Shakespeare's coattails, but he was dead beforehand. See him on a ring of Dante's Hell, with his computer on his back, counting his footnotes by hand, and farting great ugly toes for every new footnote he can't resist imagining. See him — more harrowing — as the famous professor of a famous southern university, striking his classes numb with boredom, starving his graduate students into submission, writing the books that will choke you to death.

But all this that I finally learned about scholars and scholarship was in the future — all this, the genuine fruit of my two dissertations, was to take another ten years of bitter tasting. Still I will roll it into a brick and throw it. The more selective our vision, the less we see; the more precise our vision, the less we see; the more sweeping our vision, the less we see. Knowledge I'm talking about.

Meanwhile I wrote my dissertation. I never finished that orderly second reading of the poems I had planned. I was ready to write, and did write, and turned out my six hundred pages in twelve weeks, and my adviser read them all expeditiously and carefully and enthusiastically despite his reservations. My wife and I retyped the thing to meet some criticisms, and she and I and friends of ours indexed it, and the typewriter held together till the end. So on a fine day in February I sat in an auditorium along with a few dozen other men to receive my Ph.D. I had worked hard, I had a dissertation that I thought would make a book, and I was thirty-four years old. It was this last thought that preoccupied me. To be sure I had spent two years at war after leaving my undergraduate university. There had been a year of teaching before graduate school and a half year of manual labor. There were three years of teaching during my graduate studies, and there were two novels. But still I was thirty-four, and though I was proud of what I had done, I would have been prouder if I had been twenty-four. Men should not be writing dissertations when they are thirty-four. In truth I felt embarrassed and ashamed, and I was glad to see that some of the other men were older than I.

Still I could not deny my experience, and I thought about it too. One day in the midst of my discoveries about McPherson my mother-in-law came to visit us, and she and my wife and I stood talking in the garden. It was a lovely summer day, and the unhappy home life that I once saved my girl from was nearly forgotten. We did not talk about my discoveries, for my mother-in-law was not a scholar's wife, but my discoveries were upon me like a sweet influence. We stood by a bed of roses, and I picked the loveliest rose and gave it to my mother-in-law. No rose had a thorn that day.

4

ALL PASSION SPENT TEACHING

The night before my very first class I sat in a dingy hotel gathering my thoughts upon eight-by-five note cards. The fact that I had no thoughts to gather made me extremely nervous, and I foresaw that my debut would be ignominious. In a way I realized that this must be so, just as a child must be afraid of the dark; and the only thing to do was to put on the bravest front possible. Keep talking was the instruction I gave to myself, and I managed to devise a way to last out more than twice fifty minutes. In the event, I stumbled through it all in forty-five minutes and spent the next night wondering what the future held.

It was a curious year, that first year. I had to teach grammar, about which I knew nothing, so I went to a grammar text and condensed its wisdom to essentials, and recited those essentials to my students for them to copy down. I rarely gave classroom exercises in grammar because I was afraid I would not know the answers. We also read essays, and I had furious arguments with students who failed to see that Robert Hutchins was right in condemning college football. The harder I argued, the more stubborn they were. I also spent time talking about Freud and Kierkegaard and Hart Crane, not that these men were on the program but that I was full of them. Surely if there was one thing that students ought to know it was themselves, and Freud had the key. Wasn't it a moral obligation to teach him? I also talked politics and religion, tried to make radicals out of Republicans and atheists out of Catholics. The one thing I never talked about was last night's movie. I believed too much in education to do that.

I enjoyed a lot of this, for I was opinionated and argumentative, and here was a platform. Today I wouldn't teach in such a way, at least on the surface, and most of the ideas I argued for strike me as absurd. Yet I have some doubt that I am a better teacher, except in my own conscience. What mattered to me as a student was incalculable. What matters to others seems incalculable to me. I have had students for whom I felt a natural antipathy, and I have watched them sit silently through a course with supercilious disregard. A year later I have talked with them and decided I was wrong. Likewise I have been flattered by the attentions of students, and have had to admit it was flattery. One of these latter students was a girl who sat in the front row and displayed conscientious interest in everything I said. She was an attractive girl, and since it was the time when Elizabeth Taylor was pretending to be Cleopatra, she herself was pretending to be Elizabeth Taylor. A few days after the course was over she came upon me in the library and said: "Mr. O'Toole, I didn't want to say this before, but you remind me of Richard Burton." What my class must have meant to her no serious teacher can admire. But from the beginning of my teaching to the present I have been offered tokens of appreciation that have suggested that my uneasy self had something to give away.

In my own mind, though, I was vastly dissatisfied with my teaching in my first year and for several years thereafter. I knew that Freud and politics were not my business and that I went to them in part because I had nothing to say about my business. When it came to teaching the "Ode on a Grecian Urn" I was stuck. I could give my students some facts about Keats's life, but why not give them a biography? In any event the facts were not my facts. I could paraphrase the poem and enthuse over it, but my students who liked poetry could do as much. I could dig out the allusions and the meanings of archaic words, but this was mere pla-giarism. And I could go to articles on the poem and make a mishmash of them. Surely it would be more honest to put the articles in the students' hands. The very first time I taught the poem a precocious boy raised the issue of whether the quotation at the end was meant to cover more than "Beauty is truth, truth beauty," and if so, or if not, what were the impli-cations. In years since, this issue has become a commonplace, and I know what I think of it; but that poor boy didn't so much as get from me a recital of other men's opinions, and I wouldn't have been genuinely pleased to settle for those opinions, even though they would have kept me from being embarrassed. In my next year of teaching I had to conduct a course in the history of the language, a course I never took myself and a subject on which my ignorance was nearly total. What a scramble that course was! The text we used was A. C. Baugh's, and the best thing I could have done was to send my students home to read it, but I had to earn a living if nothing else, so I bought Krapp and Mencken and half a dozen other writers on the subject and scrambled them up with Baugh.

This was always the worst part of teaching — patching together my knowledge for the day. In its pettiest form it meant that any essay I taught in freshman English had to be gone over for unknown names and foreign words so that if a student should say, "Mr. O'Toole, what is *Tarr*?" I would not have to blush. Thousands of hours I have spent doing this sort of thing, and all to little avail, for my students either didn't care or were embarrassed to show their own ignorance. But just in case some nasty student wanted to be awkward, I had my armor on.

All of this was hard work and long hours, and if much of it was wasted and misguided, there eventually came a time when I completed a lecture with a sense of triumph, having conceived it finely, wrought it finely, and seen my students respond finely — I thought. I had learned by then to be only half afraid of not knowing something, and I knew what uses I wanted to make of biography, history, and criticism. It seemed to me that my task was to open a door not to Knowledge but to perception, and that the ways of doing this were so various and unsure, so dependent upon the character of teacher and student and moment, that Knowledge itself might be a way — but not my way. This task had its own pretensions and pitfalls, but teaching never became an altogether easy exercise for me, so that my occasional triumphs did not degenerate into daily smugness. What I now cared for was that my students cared for the "Ode on a Grecian Urn." If they cared for it to begin with, all well and good, and we might enjoy it together. If they didn't care, and had no intention of caring, all well and good too. For the rest, caring might happen if I told them about Keats and Fanny Brawne. What I wanted was a sense of the desire, energy, and anguish that burn in Keats's letters to her. Thread the course of his love upon those marvelous letters, and the students might understand the man, and go to his poem with that understanding ready to be transmuted just as Keats transmuted it. I wouldn't have wanted to defend this method. It fell apart every time it became method. I wouldn't have wanted to defend the theory of poetry it seemed to rest on. For the moment I rested I was nowhere. Said Keats to Fanny: "My mind is heap'd to the full; stuff'd like a cricket ball." That is the way I had to be, and if I plotted how to use Keats's letters and did not read them for their own sake, I made a mess of it. I was playing with fire. I was rubbing several fires together and hoping not to get dry sticks.

Too often I got dry sticks. With Keats, Byron, Pope, and Donne, for whom my affinities were closest, I was reasonably lucky. But suppose even with Keats I gave a successful lecture one morning, and then had ten minutes in which to recover my composure and try again with another section of the same course. Usually I failed. And Knowledge was always getting in the way. My students often wanted it, my colleagues expected it, and who was I to see my students flunk their graduate record examinations? To this day my first class in the English survey course is a recital of facts about the Anglo-Saxon invasions of England, the language of the times, and the culture. Many of these facts come from a course I had in graduate school, and for all I know the dates are wrong. I can never remember them anyway, and each year I have to go back to my notes and force them into my head again, and each year I swear I will do something better next year. But the beginning of the fall semester always catches me unprepared. I tell the students it is medicine they have to take and things may improve later on.

As soon as I began to know the way I wanted to teach, I had to revise my ideas about examinations. I had usually enjoyed taking examinations myself, but on principle I was opposed to them. Ask any right-minded teacher, and he will tell you that at best examinations are a necessary evil. Of course he does like the examinations he himself gives because they offer the student an opportunity to think, to pull together everything from the term; and they may be a creative occasion for one or two superb students. You can make yourself sick listening to this sort of complacency from your colleagues and yourself. I remember vividly that just at the time I was seeing how I wanted to teach, a colleague told me that the only justification for the classroom was that it gave the student an opportunity to be in the presence of a civilized mind. This view was close enough to my own to put me off my dinner, for he was a dull bloodless man who was visibly in the presence of death. In any event I had given examinations in the past that were calculated to engage good students, encourage the foolish, and catch the cheaters and bluffers. Evil enough, I think, and often I did not read the papers except for borderline cases. But now I was reconsidering things, and it seemed that the best sort of examination might be a simple one of identification. If the students had learned to care for the "Ode on a Grecian Urn" they ought to be able to recognize it, recognize its special character. What else did caring mean? I would offer the students a dozen fragments of poems they had not read and ask them to identify the authors. There would be no credit given for right answers, only for the reasoning behind the answers, and I would give full credit for a wrong answer with sensitive reasoning. Each fragment was meant to be typical of its author. I gave this examination for two years. In the first year I merely told the students about it the last day of class, for the notion had just come to me; and everyone failed it miserably except for an older woman who had been writing poetry for years. The other papers made me think that I myself had failed miserably or that the examination was best given privately under a tree. One girl — a beautiful girl I often admired during my lectures — scribbled at the end of her paper: "Mr. O'Toole, I don't think I'll ever be able to say 'That's Browning!' But I loved every minute of it." What did this mean?

The next year I spent the last two class hours showing students how to go about the examination. If the passage was satirical, you had grounds for thinking of Byron; if the language and rhythm were gnarled, you might begin to think about Hopkins and Browning. The students did better this second year, but I realized that with more effort I could teach the dimmest student to sort out subjects and themes and rhyme schemes and language. I had to give up that examination, and I also modified my ideas about how to teach the "Ode on a Grecian Urn." But I did see the examination prove itself with one of my colleagues. We were at a party, and someone suggested playing guess-the-poet. I gave lines from Edna St. Vincent Millay, and this colleague guessed John Dryden. I had to laugh. You may not know as much as that man, Simon — I said to myself — but at least you're not such a fool.

5

MY FATAL MISTAKE AS A TEACHER, COMMITTED IN THE NAME OF PROGRESS

The thing about progress is that it is irresistible. I have heard presidents of the Modern Language Association lament the decline of American education, and I have heard wild applause for the lament; but I take these genuflections to the past as spurs in the race into the future. Every college program I have taught in has been better than the one before it; and though my colleagues and I have become dissatisfied with the new program, we have never gone backwards. The real cry has always been excelsior.

In my first year of teaching freshman English we used an omnibus anthology called *Modern English Readings*. It gave us *The Haystack in the Floods*, Finley Peter Dunne, Robert Hutchins, *Riders to the Sea*, and Thomas Henry Huxley. Such anthologies are used today in the remote provinces if they are used at all; and I said to my chairman, for I represented the future: Who is Finley Peter Dunne that he deserves the attention of serious people? My chairman told me that Dunne was an important figure in American social history, and my chairman was a sad wreck of a man, a walking demonstration of what happened to people who taught

Finley Peter Dunne. Presently most of us had things the way I wanted them — things high class and relevant: James Bryant Conant, Harlow Shapely, Fred Hoyle, and Bertrand Russell letting us in on the twentieth century and telling us the right way to think. Textbooks like *Toward Liberal Education* gave glimpses of the splendid debate that was going on among these people about how the century could put its best foot forward; and if enough dedicated teachers like myself helped to argue the great issues of science, education, and religion, the century would get there faster. This program exhilarated me for several years, and was subjected to its own internal progress. For soon it appeared that a mishmash of two dozen thought-provoking essays lacked the depth of one whole book by one man. It was time to try Joseph Wood Krutch, whose *The Modern Temper* gave us a single perspective on all the important issues. Those of us who were bolder risked teaching the Socratic dialogues or *Coming of Age in Samoa*, and showed our students that the issues of today had been burning for two thousand years in the Near or Far East. Those who were boldest were strictly contemporary, and taught the unique plight of modern man as witnessed by Camus.

What a faithful disciple I was to these people with simple ideas; what passion I gave to their causes; what harm I intended my students! The easiest way for me to justify my classroom in those years is to imagine that my students naturally disbelieved everything I said. At any rate, I got tired of exhorting them to accept science, humanism, existentialism, loneliness, and despair. It began to seem to me, as well as to others, that our proper concern was to analyze the rhetoric of our writers, not to imitate it. There came to hand a superb little book by Paul Haines, designed to do this sort of thing. Some of the essays in it were two pages long, some of them were positively trite, and most of them were unconcerned with great issues. Yet more subtle questions could be asked about these essays than we asked about the great issues. We would not merely follow a thought process, we would tear it apart; and if we displayed the parts, our students would acquire a detachment both philosophical and literary. They would think and write better. I got so caught up in this method that

I wrote a freshman textbook with questions that were twice as complicated as anything Haines devised.

Of course I got tired again, and others got tired, and it began to seem to us that we were failing to interest our students. Too close attention to style dried up the springs of style. A sweeping and historic change was made. We would have not one freshman English program but half a dozen, and they would each possess a unity hitherto unknown — for the old omnibus anthology had merely yielded to half a dozen selected books of essays, poetry, philosophy, fiction, and drama. One section would have comedy as a topic, another American poetry, another Socrates. The freshman would choose the topic that interested him, and for the whole semester he would be engaged by and inspired to think and write on his topic. This new approach lasted three years, when another sort of factor had to be considered. The hiring of instructors to teach freshman English was suddenly becoming difficult, for other colleges were now offering them advanced courses, and other colleges were snatching away the men we wanted to hire. Freshman English was thereupon done away with, and a first-year world-literature course substituted. And here the very summit of achievement was reached, for necessity happened to coincide with progress. We could afford to do away with freshman English because our freshmen were coming to us better prepared than ever before — the result of the general advance in American education. Imagine now the lucky instructor and his clever students leaping from peak to peak across the ages — from Homer, Sophocles, and Virgil to Kafka, Joyce, and Hemingway.

Of course the summit is merely the point from which one soars off into the wide blue yonder, but the rest of the story is the same old story, and I will end it here except to record a fall I had one day while I was mountaineering. I was teaching Virgil at the time, and my preoccupation was with values — with how Virgil felt about war and state as against how Homer felt. It seemed to be a deeper preoccupation than right-thinking or rhetoric, and I imagined that anyone who comprehended values all the way from Homer to Hemingway must be a very sophisticated person

[34

indeed. I myself was both acquiring and displaying such sophistication, for I was reading Virgil for the first time, one week ahead of my students. Personal progress went in tandem with the freshman English program. On this one day I was examining the values involved in Aeneas's leaving Dido and Carthage to found Rome, and in the midst of my exemplary discussion I saw a doubtful female hand rise, and before I could nod to the girl she burst out with her question: "But if Dido really loved him, why didn't she go to Rome with him?" It was the sort of question that adds salt to the abstract. A good teacher is glad to have such questions. But I merely belabored the girl for failing to understand what I had already said. Afterward it made a good story to amuse my colleagues with — one of those thousands of stories we tell to illustrate the fact that our best work may be sadly in vain. Who else but a home economics girl would ask such a question! Who else but a wise, subtle, and kind teacher could appreciate it! I even admitted to my colleagues that I was nonplussed at the time — as much as to say that as a rule I was never nonplussed. Yet there also troubled my mind a vision of myself as a middle-aged mountain goat prancing clumsily about the peaks while this rather nice young girl was strolling about in the pleasant lowlands. Eventually I knew I had had a fall. I began to wonder about the importance of high culture as against low culture. Was it better to be able to understand values or to be able to love? Suppose that a capacity for abstracting the values of a half-dozen cultures meant a drying up of the capacity for love. Suppose that the abstracting capacity was a fake capacity, and one's abstraction of Virgil was a death mask of him. Suppose that civilization throve not on the mountaintops but in the pleasant lowlands. Looking about at my colleagues, I saw humorless, petty, arrogant, and dull men carrying forward the banner of high civilization. Some of our students were like flowers blooming in the garden. What did we want to do but make them like us? How proud and satisfied we were whenever a bright student switched his major from physics to English. We had saved him for humanity, and we could look forward to the day when he would write footnotes with the best of us. God knows what the study of physics does to young people; but if I looked beyond the apparent pleasures and progress of freshman English to the sad results of the study of literature — to myself and my colleagues — I seemed to be looking down the road to Hell, to the mountain turned upside down.

In these reflections I made my own most recent progress as a teacher. It may not be any less foolish and arrogant and falsely modest than anything else I ever arrived at; but I thought so at the time, and I think so now. There is a room, and I am in it for an hour, and students come because they want to, have to, don't have anything better to do — for whatever reason. I teach a subject I don't know how to teach and that is unteachable. If I give my students anything, I very likely cause them equal harm. We do a dance around some poems, and sometimes it may be a pleasant dance; and if it is a pleasant dance, it may deprive the students of a desire to dance around poetry by themselves, and why should they want to dance around poetry at all if there is a boy or girl to dance with instead? Civilization can thrive without the "Ode on a Grecian Urn," and if we are glad to have the poem, we should not be so glad as to become proud and solemn. Treat the poem lightly, and enjoy it lightly in a thoughtful mood.

All this while, of course, I was making my fatal mistake. It was a simple mistake, and I cannot say I was unaware I was making it. My greatest progress as a teacher — from the time of my first successful lecture to the time of my fall — came when I was teaching at Brunch University; and my future at Brunch had nothing to do with this progress. I was spending vast quantities of energy filling the chinks in my armor, learning how to teach the unteachable, discovering what civilization isn't. I was assisting in the grand forward march of American education. But so far as my superiors were concerned, I ought to have been publishing scholarly articles.

6

HOW TO SUCCEED WITHOUT REALLY PUBLISHING

There is one easy way to succeed without publishing, and that is to become an administrator. I knew a prodigious scholar once — he was chairman of the department at Brunch University — and he had got on with very little publishing. How well I remember the cold day he invited me into his office to tell me whether I was to be promoted or fired. "I hear good things about your teaching, Simon," he said, "but . . ." A pregnant pause. "Publish." He said it gently, kindly, and I was not fired but given another year's grace in which to publish. I actually admired this man, for he had more style than most of his colleagues; and even as I looked with bitterness upon his decision, I did not blame him personally: he was obeying the universal rule of prestigious colleges. I hardly even thought to say "publish yourself" back at him. For what had he published? A freshman textbook, a few clever reviews, an article or two; that was all. And he knew — and I didn't — that his success was hollow. How could he hold his head high among his peers, or even among junior members of his own department who were publishing books fast and furiously? He was supposed to be editing the works of a nineteenth-century poet, and he had been at the task several years without visible results. Then not long after I left the university — fired the following year — his car was stolen and with it the priceless materials of a genuine success. The man did not remain department chairman. He moved on into administration, and the last I heard he was president of a large and undistinguished college, doubtless glad to consort with other men who never really published anything.

And yet publishing is not all that hard, as I myself learned, and the real fact of American scholarship is that the great majority of successful scholars squeeze through on a single scholarly book, produced in their twenties or thirties. Having bought their way into respectability by this means, they settle down to a slow piece of editing, a textbook, reviewing, or an article every two years to show that the old master still keeps in touch. The scholars for whom the writing of books is a natural labor, who do not give the task up as soon as possible, can be counted on several fingers. How many American scholars have produced ten books, how many have produced five — not anthologies, pieces of editing, textbooks, symposia, and the like, but books whose first and last words are their own?

The more extraordinary thing, of course, is how many scholars fail to produce even that first book. For most of them try, try desperately, and their failures are the high tragedies of academic life. I know several cases of promising young scholars whose very dissertations were adjudged worthy of publication, and who never brought themselves to the point of submitting their manuscripts to waiting university presses. Some of these scholars attain legendary reputations as perfectionists, mute inglorious Miltons of the academic graveyard. They have half a dozen footnotes still to write, one chapter still to mull over, one thread still to tie, before their definitive study of Crashaw is completed. And while they sit and think, other busy young people are actually squeezing out their books on Crashaw, and one day at the age of forty-five it is all up with the sitters and thinkers. They realize they have been bypassed, and the cherished piece of perfection goes into the drawer to gather dust, perhaps thankfully but also bitterly. What might have been? A little more effort, a little more hardheadedness, and a prized book would have stood on a shelf and in the stacks of libraries around the world, a source of wonderment to nonperfectionists. Only a few months ago a dissertation reviewing board of a famous university agreed that the dissertation they had just approved would mark the next great advance in studies of a certain metaphysical poet. I didn't mention to them that a friend of mine at another famous university was about ready to read proof on his own book on the same poet, which to him assuredly was the next great advance. Had he not labored mightily on it for eight years? He had. And was he to see his own brilliant light lost in the glare of another? With some luck, the other book would remain an unpublished dissertation.

I myself have published eight books within the last seven years. Of what sorts those books are, how I arrived at them, and what they cost me, I will in all honesty relate. My career began with my dissertation. Not my committee but I myself thought it was publishable — doubtless the common experience of dissertation writers and reviewers. But as I had no faith in my committee, I was not worried. I was hardheaded. I knew my committee was blind, and I knew the world was blind. I would pay to have that dissertation published if need be. The first step was to send it to Orlon University Press to see what they thought. And I had it back in short order with a note saying that it was unpublishable and that dissertation style was not book style. The note was more baffling than disappointing. Ten years later it is obvious to me what the difference is between a book and a dissertation; but then it was a mystery, and it remained a mystery I never consciously solved. How many young scholars are similarly baffled? They are taught the techniques of their trade, and then they are told something is wrong. What can it be? I went and examined several scholarly books, and concluded that I had too many footnotes. A few months later I arrived at my job at Brunch University with a revised manuscript. Half of my beautiful footnotes were gone.

Of the next four shameful years it is not easy to speak. That dissertation was my key to success at Brunch. I had no other books up my sleeve. A senior member of the department asked to see it, and word came back that he was pleased, and a few days later I was invited to share an advanced course with another senior member. Hope rose. I had a conversation with the first senior member, and he advised me not to cut up the dissertation into articles but to give it to the Brunch Press, which I did. The editor of that Press had seen the likes of me before, and he knew that I wanted him more than he wanted me.

"This your dissertation?" he said, as though it was muddy.

"Yes."

"Revised?"

"Yes."

"Heavy!" he said, weighing it in his hand. "How many copies will it sell?"

"A thousand or so?" — thinking that every college library in the country would need it.

"Three hundred."

There the interview ended, and the manuscript lay with him for four months, after which I received a letter saying that if I took the enclosed review to heart the Press would be interested to see the manuscript again. The reviewer was cruel and kind. Yes, there was diligence, originality, discipline; but the thing was also sloppy, conventional, and disorganized.

I revised the manuscript, but not before I tried a commercial press where another senior member of the department had connections. No luck, not a glimmer. I tried two other university presses, and each press had the manuscript looked at by two readers who disagreed with each other, and each press decided not to carry the matter further. Then I sent it back to the Brunch Press. In the meantime the department had invested $2,000 in me in summer research fellowships on McPherson, and they had an interest — as one man said — in seeing the book published. But the Press refused again, when their own two readers disagreed with each other. And now my time of trial at Brunch was running out. I, a good man, a better man than most of the men who were getting on, lacked the sine qua non of advancement at a prestigious university. How bitter I was! How I wished that two approving readers could have read for one press!

[40

Then before I left Brunch but not before I was fired, the book was accepted. The manuscript had gone out to another press and come back after a single reading. The review was favorable but not favorable enough. I consulted a senior member of the department, a friend with a name, and he wrote to that press to inquire whether it would consider publishing the book with a subsidy, and further that Brunch had funds to subsidize books. No mention was made of the fact that Brunch was unlikely to give funds to me. The press was interested. It wanted first to have another reading of the manuscript, and asked me to submit two names. One of the names I gave was that of a friend who happened to be teaching at a university near the press. The press chose my friend, and my friend wrote a most laudatory review, a copy of which he sent to me. The press thereupon invited me to find $2,000 to help with publication, and I did so out of my own pocket. And my cup of bitterness and shame was so full that I took very little pleasure in seeing the published book itself. By the time it was issued, I was teaching at Baraboo University, and my colleagues there envied me, and I was glad of their envy. But I knew the expense of spirit.

My other books came more easily. For two of them I was paid $2,000 apiece in advances, and I earned money on them all. They made me think that the shame of the first book really lay with the publishing world, with a civilization indifferent to scholarship, with the pressures of the academic community itself. Success proved my right to maneuver and scheme and pay. Moreover success was helped along by those actions. Doors were opened to me that might have remained closed. Why should I feel shame? Yet I do to this day — almost!

My other books don't make up as imposing a list as the number seven suggests. Four are textbooks, and two are an edition of McPherson's letters. Only the last and most recent is another scholarly book of my own making. Still I have no doubt that I could continue to publish scholarly books till Doomsday, for I have never touched the work of another scholar without finding all sorts of carelessness, inaccuracy, and blindness — such things as one might make a new book out of. But I have no intention of spending even the rest of my life in such enterprises. For I know the game is not worth the candle. I wonder: do so many scholars give up after their first book because they run out of gas, because they hate the task to begin with, or because they learn the folly of the work? Can it be the last if they persist in teaching the folly to their students? Or are they caught in the system? Ever since I began to be a successful scholar I have preached the wickedness of the publish-or-perish doctrine, but I have never slackened the pace of my own effort. What am I going to do now that I see my victory to be as hollow as that of my department chairman at Brunch?

I must end this chapter with a note on the articles I have published, for the peculiar delights of writing textbooks and editing letters deserve separate chapters. My first bit of publishing was itself a note, a note in *Notes and Queries*, on McPherson, in answer to someone else's note. At the time, I held my note in low esteem, for I was in my second year at Brunch, and this was the visible fruit of all my labors on McPherson, whereas my colleagues were publishing whole articles in important places. But now I have more affection for that squib than for anything else I have written. How innocent I was in those days! How hopeful! How despairing! That note symbolizes a lost world.

At the same time I wrote that note I had another piece of luck, though again not substantial enough to impress Brunch. That friend who later wrote the flattering review of my revised dissertation started a small mimeographed journal, and he asked me to contribute two bibliographical pieces on McPherson. I did, and so had three publications under my belt — but I was uneasy about being mimeographed. And then with panic setting in about my dissertation, I began to carve articles out of it, and before I left Brunch, though again not before I was fired, I had acceptances from two respectable journals. One of these journals said they could not spare thirty pages for my long article, and would I reduce it. I cut it in half, and after I left Brunch the other half was taken by *PMLA*, that Everest among scholarly journals. Did my department chairman at Brunch bite his nails in chagrin when he saw the article in print, realizing the stature of the man he let slip through his fingers? I think not. But no matter now.

Since then my path has been easy, and I have learned that a good article requires art, originality, and intelligence — which is not to say that most published articles possess any of these qualities. My latest article I wrote in a single evening in a burst of insight and fire (so it seemed) before I read a word of scholarship on the subject. I tacked the scholarship on in the next four months, and I shipped the article off to *PMLA* where the first august reader failed to see my point; and though the editors took it, as I infallibly knew they would, it was not before I spelled out everything in the sort of first paragraph for which *PMLA* is famous: what I am going to say, why it is worth saying, and what has been said before — a program fit to keep scholarly discourse at the level of high school debate.

And I wonder how many readers have picked up that article of mine and been dismayed by the opening paragraph, or worse yet, by the whole article. On principle I myself do not read scholarly articles unless I have to. The thought of sitting down and spending a pleasant hour with *PMLA*, *JEGP*, or *ELH* has never yet occurred to me, and when I do read an article it is merely as a stone to sharpen my own opinions on. I keep saying to myself: how dull, how utterly dull; the man must indeed have done it stone by stone. And yet it is difficult to believe that anyone writes an article that way. There must be insight and fire, some sort of juice in the veins. Why are the end products so gray? Can it really be called publishing?

7

DID I WIN FRIENDS AND FAME AND MAKE
A MINT WITH MY TEXTBOOKS?

Imagine, if you will, two young instructors basking in the prestige of Brunch University. One is a mere thirty-six years of age (Simon O'Toole himself), the other is in his late twenties. Men from lesser institutions tremble at their sight. The time is Saturday evening, and they sit at ease smoking the friend's cigars. Their freshman themes are corrected, their Monday classes prepared. Their devoted wives hover in the background. They bask. "Simon," says the friend, "you and I ought to do a controlled-research text." Now in those years the controlled-research text was a rather new thing — a flimsy pamphlet selling for a dollar or so, knocked together in a couple of weeks, and originally used at colleges that did not possess libraries. With a 10 percent royalty and sales of 20,000 copies each autumn (the rumored level of sales of the most popular of such pamphlets), Simon and his friend would pocket $2,000 a year for a few years.

Is anyone surprised that the conversation of these two intellectual giants does not concern the profound thoughts of the week that have lain submerged in the bustle and worry of work, and that now might float into the air along with the cigar smoke? But there is a surprise, for the friend's sentence has a character that only a scholar who knows his texts and contexts can define: an air of gentle melancholy and resignation. Simon's friend is not interested in money, he is not interested in controlled research. He is acknowledging to Simon their mutual failure at Brunch. No young scholar who sees true success coming his way will spend two minutes on such ephemera as controlled-research texts. Simon's friend is thinking of the day when he and Simon will take themselves hat in hand to the chairmen of the departments at Moccasin State Teachers College and Baraboo University. The likes of such chairmen will appreciate controlled-research texts.

"Why not?" says Simon. So they pull on their cigars. The friend thinks of one idea for such a pamphlet and Simon thinks of another idea, and in the next week they mail proposals on both to several publishers, and presently they have interested replies on Simon's idea. They knock together the pamphlet. And Simon, poor Simon, has the pleasure of holding his first book in his hands a few months before he makes his ignominious departure from Brunch.

Almost a book, and almost his. The rest of the story about that pamphlet is itself so ignominious that I would just as soon keep my distance from Simon. But I will merely put the best face on it and say that as I conceived the idea, so I elaborated it, and my perfectionism and hardheadedness were what took my friend and me four months to do the job instead of two weeks. My luckless friend, he was no perfectionist, and simply wanted to get the thing done. I made us read every scrap of literature on the subject. And during this time a terrible thought began to gnaw in the rest of my intellectual head, namely that my friend's name began with C. Was I in times to come to enter libraries across the country and find that pamphlet catalogued not under O'Toole but under C———? I was. Ah well, we all have ignominious thoughts. My friend, for instance — did he harbor a secret pleasure in the fact that his name began with C? Was he resisting an honest impulse to say to me: "Simon, it's your baby, and your name ought to come first"? For a few months, and for some while after the manuscript went off to the publisher, I fed on such thoughts. Finally I broached the subject, and my friend said that since the notion of our doing a pamphlet was his, he thought the proprietary rights were equal. Besides . . . But I leave the rest of the discussion buried. We quarreled, in a gentlemanly way. It took another textbook for us to get around to basic words.

Looking back upon that pamphlet I can see that it illustrates the guiding principle that nothing fails like success. I seized my opportunities, and my opportunities bit my hand. Hardly had my friend and I signed the contract for that pamphlet when I decided to do another text. A door had opened almost without a try. I would tear it off its hinges. My years of teaching freshman English had taught me that I could prepare a freshman anthology superior to anything else on the market. Admittedly such an anthology was still not enough to impress the chairman of the department at Brunch, except to remind him of his own failure to publish anything more substantial himself. But it could do one thing a controlled-research text could not: it could earn a pile of money. Say the text sells for $3.00, and sells 50,000 copies a year, an altogether plausible figure with freshmen enrollments around the country reaching several hundred thousands. At 15 percent royalty the editors will earn $22,500 a year for five, even ten years. Editors, not editor, for such books are usually done in collaboration, usually by two men at different universities so as to catch two likely markets. But I didn't know anyone at another university with whom I wanted to collaborate. I asked C if he wanted to do it.

I drew up a proposal and sent it off, and soon an editor from a famous publishing house was winging his way to Brunch University to drink with us one evening, to size us up, and to try to get away with a 10 percent royalty. He was an astute and civilized man, and his travelers later told me that he had an infallible nose for a good selling text. He drank brandy — Courvoisier (a name that I, poor country lad, only vaguely recognized); and C had something else distinguished, for he was a city boy who knew about liquor and cigars; and I had Calvert and ginger

[46

ale. But that editor and I got along, and I knew the contract was firm even though we did not settle down to discussing it until the next morning. How C and I sped home that night to our devoted wives; how we all hugged ourselves in advance; how we laughed at my Calvert and ginger ale!

The next morning there was a problem. Did we want a hard-cover book or a paperback? The paperback cataclysm in textbooks was just starting, and dignified people still liked cloth. Did not our chairman have the most weighty of cloth bindings to his anthology, and were we to count ourselves less than him? Our editor gave us the facts. Say the University of California wanted copies for 10,000 freshmen a year for three years. In cloth, total sales might be 13,000, for most copies would be resold for the second and third years. In paperback designed to fall apart in several months, total sales would come near to 30,000. The higher price of the cloth edition could not make up for this advantage of paperback. So C and I resisted dignity. Our editor then made an allusion to a 10 percent royalty and we made an allusion to other interested publishers, and the contract arrived a few days later with a royalty rising to 15 percent after the first 15,000 copies were sold. In point of fact, C and I knew nothing about royalties, and our allusion was a lucky accident. We would have taken 10 percent gladly. To this day I have little idea of how typical my contracts are, or whether publishers skin their academic writers on all contracts. Royalties and sales are one of the mysteries of life. I will tell all I know presently.

It was at this time in my scholarly career that I began to cheer up. Two textbooks to prepare, a dissertation that was looking halfway publishable, and a few articles in the offing. I didn't have any hope of staying at Brunch, but I would be wearing my hat when I went to Baraboo. Observe me cheered up: driving myself into labors that in the next eight years would turn my face gray.

I wrote introductory discussions for our freshman anthology. They seemed to me to be lucid and thorough. I drafted exercises that were more complicated than such exercises ever were before — designed to steer the student along a line of reasoning till he saw things exactly as I saw them. If today I cannot bear to look at that book, so bad it seems, so mistaken in its pedagogy, I did give it the best effort I knew how to give then. I think C was alarmed at what I was doing, and he managed to control my worst excesses, but I pushed all too much past him. I myself was alarmed at what our editor might think when he saw the completed manuscript, but he was as pleased as I was. For a commercial man he was highly uncommercial. Every question that arose about the way we were doing things was met with the same piece of advice: consider the criticism, and accept it only if you want to; the book is yours, not somebody else's, and it won't be worth anything unless you make your own decisions. Never was there a suggestion that if we did things that way instead of this we might sell more copies. The completed manuscript presently went to a copy editor with principles of his own, and he cut my style to pieces. Consider, said our editor, and I considered and restored my style to itself.

All this time, I being myself and no one else, another thought was gnawing in my head. Was I, who conceived the book and who was doing the essential work on it, and who might want to subsidize my study of McPherson and perhaps even retire from academic life for two years to regain my composure — was I to share royalties equally with my friend? Let me say, not in my defense but for the sake of friendship everywhere, that when two friends undertake a commercial task together they ought to have an unpleasant preliminary discussion of selfish issues. Such an unpleasantness will forestall a greater. My friend and I were high-minded at the outset, and we had our due reward. I eventually raised the subject, and my friend called me a name that makes an imperfect rhyme with the name of my odious Professor Puck. Our friendship was broken, but the glories to be won with the anthology were too great for either of us to resist going on. I took six-tenths of the royalties, and we completed the book and never smoked his cigars together again.

Very soon after that book was completed, there came a letter from our editor saying that the introductions were so splendid that he wondered whether we would write a rhetoric for him. Now a rhetoric is to a freshman anthology as a freshman anthology is to a controlled-research text. The best selling rhetoric in the land reportedly had sales of 150,000 copies a year, and it was then more than twenty years old. Its two chief rivals reportedly sold above 100,000 each, and they likewise had been going on for some while. Suppose a rhetoric were written to end all rhetorics. Would not the editors become exceedingly rich exceedingly fast? My friend, being some years younger than I and having more hope of scholarly advancement, decided against becoming a millionaire. He left the book to me, and it was revealed to our editor that I was the author of the glittering introductions. The editor was satisfied, and there I was with the whole cake to myself.

The time was a time of crisis for rhetorics. Everyone used the standard rhetorics — fat stodgy books full of unreadable exercises — and everyone hated them except their authors. Only a year or two before, E. B. White came across a slender style guide that he had used at Cornell University more than thirty years before, and he wrote a graceful introduction to it and updated a few points of usage, and it leaped into sales of over 100,000 a year despite being altogether inadequate for the modern freshman course. The reason was hatred of the standard rhetorics. My uncommercial editor and I saw what was needed — a book to fall between the few dozen pages of White's guide and the six hundred pages of the standard rhetoric; moreover a book with some of White's grace. Could I do it? My editor gave me $2,000 for a start, and I went at the task with all my wits. In the course of doing it, my editor invited me to a small dinner in honor of a textbook writer whose single book had sold a million copies in thirty years. There was much talk at the dinner about his Cadillac and his swimming pool, much easy laughter about the trials and tribulations of writing and publishing. I was going to leave that man far behind. When I departed from Brunch University, a failed scholar, I comforted myself with the thought that in three or four years I would be drinking champagne while my former colleagues would still be laboring in their barren vineyards.

I can read that rhetoric I wrote to this day. I pick it up and chuckle over bits and pieces. True there are dull parts, confusing parts; but most of what is wrong is that the book is too good — that's what I think. It was a failure. I had a letter from a teacher who delighted in it the way I delighted in it; but silence otherwise. I did one more freshman text after that, and here are the facts and figures about them all. In every case I gratefully accepted a contract that the publisher himself devised, and I am sure that almost every academic author does the same. In two cases I pressed for advances against royalties, and got them. In the first case there was every reason for the publisher to have offered me one to begin with, for there were negligible permission costs.

Controlled-Research Text. Paperback. 10 percent royalty throughout, on 75 percent of the published price. No advance. Permission costs of $722, requiring sales of 5,000 copies before earnings began (the publisher paying the sum and repaying himself out of the first royalty returns). Price originally $1.75, rising to $2.25.

Year	Sales
1	5,000
2	4,600
3	2,450
4	7,100
5	3,250
Total	22,400

Royalties of $2,400 were earned after permissions.

Freshman Anthology. Paperback. 10 percent royalty on the first 10,000 copies, 12½ percent royalty on the next 5,000, 15 percent thereafter — on the published price. No advance. Permission costs of $3,000, requiring sales of 10,000 copies before earnings began. Price $2.95, rising to $3.75.

Year	Sales
1	11,000
2	11,000
3	11,000
4	5,200
5	2,200
Total	40,400

Royalties of $16,500 were earned after permissions.

Rhetoric. Cloth. 10 percent royalty on the first 10,000 copies, 12½ percent on the next 10,000, 15 percent thereafter — on the published price. Advance of $2,000. Permission costs of $20. Sales of 6,800 copies needed before further earnings began. Price $3.00, rising to $3.75.

Year	Sales
1	5,700
2	9,900
3	5,100
4	1,500
Total	22,200

(A single university bought upwards of 7,000 copies in the second year and 3,000 in the third.) Royalties of $8,000 were earned including the advance.

Another Freshman Text. Paperback. 10 percent royalty on the first 10,000 copies, 15 percent thereafter — on the published price. Advance of $2,000. Permission costs of $3,200. Sales of 15,000 copies needed before further earnings begin. Price $3.00.

Year	Sales
1	1,900
2	1,600
Total	3,500

No royalties were earned beyond the advance. The book appears to be a dead loss to publisher and author alike. The advance paid for about a thousand hours of work to produce the book.

None of the books came near my expectations, but how they fared in comparison with other textbooks is another story, and I wish I knew more about it. I suspect two things: that publishers encourage teachers — potential writers — to believe that top sales are higher than they are, and that I had more than average success all told. I worked hard for what I got. One does not write two hundred and fifty pages of even a bad rhetoric overnight, and if I translated my reward into an hourly rate of pay, I would make no one envious but a poor man. Doubtless there are fortunes to be made in textbooks, and why shouldn't anyone with a bright idea or a dull one have a try? But he ought to know that his chances are slender. The few hard facts I have about textbooks other than my own are that almost all of them have been failures, earning their authors and editors either nothing or one or two thousand dollars. Two have been very considerable successes. The publishers make their own fortunes on a few books, and make repeated stabs at new fortunes. They cannot be so optimistic as their authors except when they talk to their authors. Or can they? What are the benefits to a publisher of a failed text such as my rhetoric? Twenty thousand copies, say, at $3.00. Royalty to author of 10–12½ percent, and discount of 30 percent to the college book stores. Total income to publisher of $35,000. He has printed 25,000 copies altogether, given away 3,000 to teachers at the start and been left with 2,000 at the end. There has to be an editor, copy editor, designer, salesman, secretary, office, and warehouse. There are manufacturing costs. Say the publisher has no string to his bow in the way of one or two regular successes but has to rely on producing a dozen such failures every four years. Twelve times $35,000 divided by four for his yearly income of $105,000. Is he in business or not? I never got around to asking my editor, who might have been hurt by such a question. In the end he seemed to be angry with me anyway. Was it because I was the wrong horse he had backed? Or did he get out of me exactly what he thought was likely?

In my dreams there is one more textbook that I am going to write. The publisher will approach me to do the job, and we will have a cat and mouse game of negotiating. I will be the cat, and I will name impossible terms to see whether they are possible — say 25 percent royalty from the outset rising to 40 percent after the sale of 40,000 copies. I will be agreeable to taking 20 percent or 15 percent or 10 percent if the publisher shows me that for him to write a contract at 11 percent or 16 percent or 21 percent will be unwise for him and for all his other authors. The negotiating will be done over Courvoisier and a good cigar. We will also agree that every royalty statement will show who has bought the text and how many copies he bought, for in the past I have felt it an awkward matter to have to ask for such information. And then having settled all pettiness in advance, my publisher and I will produce a gem of a book and will remain friends forever. If the book does not sell a million copies, that will not matter, for it is only a dream.

Not long ago my friend C and I prepared a second edition of our freshman anthology. Our editor gave us directions. The introductions to the first edition were verbose and flippant, the exercises unintelligible. Change all that. Certain selections had offended Catholic colleges. Change them. Do not consider; change! O uncommercial man, you became commercial even as I became commercial. I produced that first edition with excellence in view before money, and in time found my excellence appalling. Surely I could do worse in the second edition than to write for money first and last. My friend acquiesced. But I never really knew about my friend. All along he may have had much the purest heart of the three of us.

8

THE POLITE, DULL, AND HYSTERICAL ART OF
EDITING LETTERS. PRELIMINARIES

Was there ever a methods of research seminar — the great introductory course in graduate schools — that instructed future editors of letters in how to hold hands with mad relatives of famous authors? Not that the relatives I dealt with were mad. No, it was I who was mad. But I wish I had had such a seminar. I might instead have gone off and won my scholarly fame by doing something pleasant, like committing suicide.

The curse upon me was my thoroughness. If a fact lay three thousand miles across the floor, I was willing to crawl for it. If a piece of dead wood lay three thousand miles beneath the tree of Knowledge, I was willing to dig. Observe me flexing my muscles for such an exercise. I am at Brunch University, and casting about for a quick success — an article or two that cannot fail of publication, and the only such articles I know are those that deal with original manuscript material. I learn that McPherson's aged sister has died in the house in Sussex where McPherson lived out his last years, and that the papers in the house have come into the possession of her daughter. I suspect that the shoeboxes in the closets contain valuable documents, and I write to the daughter and tell her that Brunch University and I might be interested in buying whatever turns up. Save every scrap of paper, even laundry bills, I say to her, for I see that I may be able to decipher a fragment of McPherson's marital life from his dirty linen. But the daughter writes to me presently that she has built a bonfire of all the papers. What a wicked woman that is, I think, not to take an American scholar seriously, not to let me write an article for *PMLA*. Today — oh today I wish she might have burned all of McPherson's letters in that splendid fire.

In broad outline, though, everything went according to the rules, and I bought my fame in storybook fashion. When I was writing my dissertation I picked up stray facts about McPherson's life, and I soon knew that the two biographies of him were full of holes and that several thousand letters of his lay scattered across England, America, and South Africa. If I could write a true life, or if I could edit those letters, I would be a famous scholar — not merely one of five dozen writers of critical studies of him but a man irrevocably associated with his name for all the gray years of eternity, and Harvard or Yale might be honored by my presence. But this was not a hope, it was an awareness of the facts of life. As long as I lived in the scholarly world, I wanted success in it, wanted the salves to the ego that success brings. I knew contemptible men about me, and they were able to look on me with contempt. It needed to be vice versa. But I had no positively pleasant dream of being a distinguished professor at Harvard. I would be that only if I had to be, and only if I could avoid the nightmare of being an undistinguished professor at some nameless college. There was no future I foresaw that I wholeheartedly wanted. So the thought of that life and those letters lay in the recesses of my mind, inching forward with each small item on McPherson that I published, taking a first giant step on the day I paid $2,000 toward the publication of my critical study, becoming an armed vision when I signed my contract for the letters with an illustrious university press, and sitting now like a monster on my heart.

See me at the outset of my venture, conversing in a garden in Sussex on a summer day. The garden looks out upon the Weald, that loveliest of lowlands, and I drink my tea and do not object to the scholarly life. Brunch University has given me $1,000 to come to England to look for drafts of McPherson's poems, and the daughter of McPherson's sister, whose wickedness lies in the future, is telling me that she knows nothing of their whereabouts. We chat inconsequentially for another half-hour and I am ready to leave. Then she says: "Mr. O'Toole, I do not like to talk about Uncle. I wish he were deader than dead, but I think you ought to be told the things that someday will have to be told publicly." I shiver with foreknowledge of those holes in the biographies, and the niece drives her Jaguar through them. McPherson was blackmailed for several years by a postal clerk. He was not the father of his three children. He was murdered, and his wife committed suicide.

Now McPherson is not Henry James, but he is worth almost as much as John Ruskin on the academic scales, and the sensation caused by the revelations about Ruskin's marriage would be as nothing compared with the cuckolding and murder of McPherson. The Weald fades from view, and the niece gives me the facts.

"You've not met McPherson's sons," she says. "When you do, notice their pointed ears. The same as mine."

I examine her ears.

"The same as my father's. The same as my brother's. There are no such pointed ears on the McPherson side, except in McPherson's sons. My brother, young as he was, was the father. . . . You must meet my brother, but do not say you have seen me. He's a success, my brother is, but unreliable. Drinks. . . ."

I leave the Weald full of new facts that complement my own facts, and during the next weeks I become Henry James myself, peering from behind keyholes into other people's lives and sifting my imperfect vision. I visit the brother in his office in Richmond. He is a gynecologist and will give me half an hour of his time. What can I learn in half an hour aside from the shape of his ears? We talk, and he says nothing, and I rise to leave, and he says come and see the view from the roof. We go to the roof and look out upon the Thames, and I say goodbye, and he says come down and see Richmond Green. We go down to see the Green, and I say goodbye, and he suggests we have a drink.

Thereupon I seem to be faced with a moral dilemma hitherto unknown to scholars. Shall I get this man drunk and let him confess his sins? Shall I even prompt the confession? And after such despicable behavior, will I be fit to write a decent sensational biography? Such questions do me credit until I realize that I have only five shillings in my pocket, hardly enough to set the man on his course. I can only hope that he and I will meet again when I am richer and have solved the moral issue.

In the pub he orders a double gin, downs it in a gulp, and orders another. Presently I explain my financial state, and he is gracious about it, and says that when we leave the pub I will come to his club for lunch. So we have half a dozen double gins apiece, and we go around to his club and have a bottle of champagne for a starter and another bottle during the meal. Now I hold my liquor badly, and six double gins alone can put me to sleep or make me vomit. But if my man is to drink, I must drink; and if he is to get usefully drunk, I must keep my wits about me. Has ever scholar been so sorely tried, even after he has let the moral issue slip by?

I undertake delicate questions: "Was McPherson's wife really beautiful?"

"A mag — magnificent specimen of humanity." He makes a drunken but understandable gesture. "Sumptuous."

"You liked her."

"Hated her guts."

"But a mag — magnificent specimen."

"Ho, ho, ho," we say together, and he pokes a finger at me.

"Visited me at Canterbury."

"Alone?"

"When the old man made his annual trips to South Africa."

"What did she want?"

"Ho, ho, ho."

Jamesian thrust: "What did *you* want?"

"Ho, ho, ho."

I never get any further than that with him. In the end it seems like a game: how drunk can we both get without sliding over the border beyond the outrageously suggestive? A few weeks later I give him a return engagement at Simpson's, where we drink three bottles of champagne courtesy of Brunch University; but it is a repeat performance except for McPherson's death.

"Something covered up about that," I say.

"Oh she killed him, that's what's covered up. Drove him to it. On his deathbed she didn't give him peace. Killed herself with a heart attack two days later."

"I heard something about overdoses . . ."

"You've been talking to my sister. A bit unstable, my sister. Must have told you a fancy tale about a postal clerk too."

I spend the rest of the summer with other relatives and acquaintances. They all think each other queer, and they all have different facts. I take everything down, and it is a Jamesian marvel. Still I seem to arrive at the truth, just as poor Lambert Strether finally sees with his own eyes. McPherson's former gardener tells me that one day he came upon the old man giving it to her, and nine months later she was delivered of the first child. There is, I finally decide, no truth whatever in the revelations, and I go home to Brunch without either scandal or drafts. I never do manage to meet McPherson's sons, who live mainly in South Africa. I hope by now they are dead.

Still that summer had its uses, and anyone who intends to write lives and edit letters in spite of my experience will be glad to know that my moral dilemma worried me unduly. Not that I want to exonerate myself, but I came to realize that McPherson's relatives had been lying in wait for me. Fourteen years had passed since McPherson's death, fourteen years in which hardly anyone had let them uncork their feelings and fantasies. How the niece must have gloated at the thought of getting me down on my back on the Weald! How the nephew must have feared that I would abandon him at his office, on the roof, on Richmond Green, in the pub!

[58

Does ever a scholar invade the privacy of the family of his famous author? I think not. I see them waiting impatiently for him to turn up, with individual schemes for getting him drunk.

At any rate I returned to England the following summer without shame. My eye was now on the letters, for I realized that a biography whether scandalous or sober would take years to write, whereas I could dash off a collection of letters in no time. Quick fame was the spur, and a hitherto elusive cousin of McPherson's was the instrument. She happened to own a thousand letters, and also acted for the eldest son, who held the copyright to all the letters. Without her I was nowhere. I found her, and we met on a Saturday afternoon in a hotel in Battersea. She was in her sixties then, and looked like Ethel Barrymore, with a fine strong face, great beauty of eyes and expression, and remarkable vigor. She was twenty years younger than McPherson, and she was doubtless the one person in or out of his family he deeply loved. And however much I came to regret my professional involvement with her, it was an unforgettable moment when she walked into the hotel lounge out of the past, someone whose glamorous image of forty years before was known to me and who had shared some of the life of the admirable McPherson.

She and I got along immediately. She talked and I listened. She was, I think, a person more interested in nuance than Henry James himself, and our conversation was like Henry James talking to himself — she meditating and ruminating in great flights of memory and association, and I myself bent in a fixed position at the keyhole. She talked for two hours, and then she trotted me across to a public library to find a passage in one of the poems, and kept me standing there an hour while she failed to find it, talking all the time. An indefatigable woman she was; and though I was numb afterward, I liked her. Of course I wanted to like her. Doubtless she wanted to like me. Doubtless we both wanted to ingratiate ourselves. We seemed to succeed. No mention was made of the letters on that occasion, but after a few more similar sessions it was agreed that I should edit them subject to her approval of the manuscript.

One more summer of my life was gone, and my advance toward the letters was matched by an academic retreat. I was now fired from Brunch, and took up my post at Baraboo. My next task with the letters was to get the permission of the libraries to use their holdings, and then to find a publisher, and it seemed to me that the very name of Baraboo would frighten everyone away. I was wrong. Very likely my path would have been a trifle smoother if I had been a famous man at a famous university, but I told the libraries of the cousin's cooperation and alluded to my articles and my silently subsidized book, and the answers were courteous and agreeable, except from a single library in the West. This library, founded upon gold and situated in the middle of a desert, said they would not let me use their letters, would not let me have copies of the letters, would not tell me what letters they had except that all their McPherson manuscripts were contained in several boxes. The boxes were being used by a graduate student there who had sole right to them for the next eighteen months, and the library was willing only for me to come out and take a look at the boxes without a pencil in my hand. I wrote back that my doctor did not allow me to fly. Would they tell me something about those boxes so that I could decide whether a train trip of three thousand miles was worth while? They would not.

I did not know then that this library was a feared and hated institution among civilized people, an upstart library that in the past twenty years had leaped ahead of venerable eastern libraries in its manuscript holdings. Years afterward I talked with one of the haters, a female, who told me that the buyer for the upstart library learned his trade in her own New England offices. A few years ago, she said, when a manuscript came on the market it went to the library whose collection it most suited. We would call up the New York Public Library, the Morgan Library, Harvard — she named others — and decide who should make the bid; but today the prices are fantastic, and that vile man bids on whole catalogues. I commiserated with the poor woman. I did not suggest that her own manuscripts belonged by right in the British Museum, and I did not tell her that the upstart library was merely lonely and wanted to be loved. For I did make my trip to the desert, and surrendered myself — a genuine living scholar from the fabled East — and the library thereupon surrendered the letters to me with little ado. It was like that always: patience, tenacity, a willingness to crawl three thousand miles across the floor, and I had the thing I wanted. In due course I received copies of thousands of McPherson's letters from fifty libraries, and I made a selection and sent it off to a distinguished university press. The answer came on my fortieth birthday. "O Simon O'Toole," I said to myself — "O Simon O'Toole, Assistant Professor of English at Baraboo University, you will not be here long!"

9

THE POLITE, DULL, AND HYSTERICAL ART OF
EDITING LETTERS. CONSUMMATION

The British Museum Newspaper Library is situated far along the reaches of the Northern Underground Line, in a dismal and nondescript suburb of London. I have stumbled out of that library at noontime, blind with fatigue, and sought a decent restaurant in which to hang my head for half an hour, and never found it, but found squalid cafés and squalid pubs set along mean streets; and I have settled for a bar of Bourneville Chocolate and stumbled back into that library, which looks from the outside as though it ought to be burning newspapers instead of housing them. Occasionally in my wanderings I have seen gliders in the sky — on Saturday afternoons when a scent of country air sweeps across the hill where the library stands — and I have looked up at the gliders and wondered why I am dying here.

The library inside is clean, well lighted, comfortable, and the service is courteous and efficient. But be warned, American scholar, the efficiency is English efficiency; it is formal and deliberate; and if you tell the attendants that you are in a hurry and want special service because you have traveled three thousand miles and have less time and more importance than the natives, be sure that you will have your knuckles rapped. Some American scholars need only be their normal ingratiating selves to receive such treatment. They will want to die in a hurry, and the attendants will have them die by inches.

I flatter myself that I have died both ways. I made a mistake when I negotiated my contract to edit McPherson's letters. I arranged that the first volume would be a special collection of letters to McPherson's mother, and the second volume a general collection. McPherson was a faithful son, and his mother saved every letter he wrote to her from the time he was five years old, and these letters deserved a volume to themselves. I made it the first volume because I could dash it off more quickly than the general volume. What I failed to realize was that McPherson's first ten years as a struggling author — a subject hitherto unexplored by scholarship — were a common subject of his letters to his mother. "Dearest Mother," McPherson wrote on April 1, 1894, "You recall that piece of mine in the *Liverpool Weekly Mercury* I showed you some while back. . . ." What piece, and when was some while back? As possessor of wisdom and writer of footnotes I had to know, and the way to know was to turn the pages of the *Liverpool Weekly Mercury* from October 1, 1893, to March 1, 1894. There was a certain thrill in doing this, in seeing advertisements for electropathic belts, Apollinaris Water, and Pears' Soap, and then coming upon McPherson's name. I developed a skill at it, an ability to scan a page of newspaper print at a glance and catch McPherson's name buried in the smallest type in a corner. Whether it was intuitive, telepathic, or mechanical, I cannot say; but it was genuine; and it would have saved me enormous quantities of time except that I never quite trusted it. For there were occasions when I turned the pages from October to March and found nothing, tried again and found nothing, tried from April to April and found nothing. Was I blind? Or, as dawned on me after a while, did the library have only the Five Star edition on the day McPherson's piece appeared, and McPherson's piece appeared in the Four Star edition? And there were poems and essays that McPherson merely said he sold to a newspaper syndicate, and the newspaper syndicate could sell them to whoever among two thousand newspaper proprietors wanted to buy them. Take a guess, and try ten provincial newspapers in Sussex over a period of a year. Find nothing. It was thrilling to do for two days, but two days became two weeks, two months, two summers. It was a job for a moron, and because I wanted fame, I became a moron. Presently my hair began to fall out, and eventually the job was done.

Other jobs I could do in my armchair at home. That reference of McPherson's to a character in a Beresford novel — what were Beresford's dates, and could I sum up Beresford in a phrase and identify which of all his novels McPherson was alluding to, doing this in a casual footnote as though I had read all the man's novels as a matter of course several years before editing McPherson's letters? Certainly I could, and I did the likes of this three hundred times, until my manuscript was an impregnable fortress. No matter that I never did read one of Beresford's novels. I went to a biographical dictionary of authors for his dates and summing up, and obtained his three most recent novels preceding the date of McPherson's reference, glanced at the first one and found the name, and there I was with my footnote. Done in a trice sometimes, and no one was the wiser, not even myself.

I did have lighter moments. I found a cockroach in my soup at the august Reform Club in London where I was given lunch by an old friend of McPherson's. I listened to unprintable facts about McPherson's sex life from another old friend — ordinary facts but told in an unprintable way. And I visited a famous singer whose guest book rang with the names of Lawrence, Shaw, Einstein, Tito, Toscanini, and now rings with the name of Simon O'Toole. She had been a beautiful young woman when McPherson knew her in middle age, and she was sixty when I came to see her. Over the telephone she said: "The letters are under the piano; we'll have a scramble there together." But she was a professional virgin. She greeted me at the door in flaming red dress and dyed black hair, struck a pose, and said: "Do you know, I was just thinking of the last thing he ever said to me. It was [and she threw back her head and paused to think]

[64

it was — Proust would have liked you. No, no, it wasn't that; it was —
Proust would have *loved* you." Do you mean to say you never met Proust?
I should have demanded; but I did not know the likes of this woman
among the wives of my colleagues. We went into her sitting room, and
covering the walls from top to bottom were original paintings by every
notable French and English painter of the twentieth century. Gifts to her
beautiful self, for which there was nothing given in return. There on a
table was the famous guest book. And there under the piano were two
black boxes filled with a fortune in letters, of which the two hundred
from McPherson were a modest part. We drank tea, and talked about
McPherson and his wife. "He wasn't in love with her," she said. "Wasn't
he?" I said. "He was in love with another woman," she said. "Who?" I
said. "Why me," she said.

After two years of such work I completed the research on the first
volume. I then made my final selection of letters from the whole vast
number of filial letters, postcards, and notes; and I sent a copy of it off
to the cousin for her approval. In another month the manuscript would
be ready for the publisher, and nine months after that I would be famous.
But the cousin wrote back that the letters weren't nice letters at all, and
showed McPherson didn't love his mother as he ought, and must not be
published; and when I came over to England next summer she would
show me the few letters that were tolerable and that could be slipped into
the general volume; and how was that volume progressing? Dear lady,
for some while now she had been concluding her letters to me "with
love," and she concluded this one with love too. And I, who was very
fond of her but diffident about giving my love in letters, now for the
first time concluded a letter to her with love. I was gray with rage, but
she was not going to destroy my work and my hopes.

We argued the matter by letter for the next few months, while the
illustrious press waited patiently. I pointed out that I had spent a few
thousand pounds and several thousand hours doing the work; that she
had known the tenor of the collection from the excerpts published in
the biographies; and that she had expressed enthusiasm for this special

volume. In all conscience . . . In all conscience she was a principled woman, and the full force of McPherson's actual dislike of his mother — for that is what it came to — did not strike her, and could not have struck her, until she read the six hundred letters in my selection. She was dreadfully sorry for me, but I had made a dreadful mistake, a mistake essentially of taste, and no misguided notions of academic scholarship would persuade her to change her mind. With love.

Some months later I sailed for England and we met and kissed, and I said that if the volume to the mother was not published, I would drop the project entirely. This surprised her. It upset her. Would I at least be willing to see the other volume published first? But no, I said, I had lost too much time; and I gave her a thumbnail sketch of the scholarly life in America. She then agreed to have her literary agent read the letters, and if the literary agent thought they should be published, we would go ahead with them. I went back to my London flat and waited, and the agent eventually reported in my favor, and I went and drank tea with the cousin and we agreed that the agent was a splendid man with impeccable taste. The cousin then confessed that she had not read beyond the first fifty letters in the copy I sent her. She had been so distressed by them.

This was the climax. It was all clear sailing after that except for the anticlimax two months later. I went to visit the cousin one evening and we sat in the gathering gloom while she told me one of her long stories about McPherson, a story I had heard before and was not attending to. Instead I was attending to the gloom, which was positively entering our presence. Twilight fell, and night was falling, and still the cousin turned no lights on. When we could barely see one another she said in a low voice that the letters to the mother must not be published. She had finally got around to reading them all, and though she respected her literary agent, some sort of momentary blindness, perhaps kindness to me, had deluded the agent. How I weathered this new storm is not worth telling, but weather it I did, weather-beaten to the core, and after several more months I held the published volume in my hand.

The rest of the tale makes me weep, it is so true to the dream of

[66

American scholarship. Three months after the volume was published, I had a letter from a famous old editor of letters asking me if I would come and take over his courses next term at his famous old university, a university one speaks of in such hushed terms that it hardly needs to be named. For private reasons I did the unimaginable and declined the offer. Thereupon I had another letter spelling things out. Come look us over for the term, the famous old man said, and decide if you want to stay with us; you will teach a mere four hours a week and be paid what will amount to $200 an hour, and have an assistant to help correct papers; and moreover I saw so-and-so last night and the Guggenheim Fellowship is a certainty for you.

Did I yield? I yielded. On a cold day in January I attended a session of his graduate seminar, preparatory to taking it over. Four students sat in comfortable chairs in his office ready to deal with an eighteenth-century novel that I had always meant to read and never did read until the week before. To one side of us were logs in a grate, unlighted logs, unlighted I think since 1932 when the building was built in imitation of Oxford where they use fires. The two-hour session began with a sweet intense girl reading a paper in a sweet intense voice, and when she was done the famous old scholar said that it was a very interesting paper, Janet, but you were a bit nervous and read too fast. Any comments by anyone? One boy said that in the future it would be helpful to have outlines of the papers being read. Any other comments? No other comments. The famous old scholar then drew out some old notes and asked Janet what she had made of the epigraphs to each of the seventy-five chapters of the novel. Janet had pre-occupied herself with the images of the novel, and made nothing of the epigraphs, so the famous old scholar read a few epigraphs and told us that three were by Shakespeare, two by Montaigne, four by Dryden; and if there were no more comments that was all for today. He put a hand on my shoulder as we left, and I felt the mantle of wisdom settling upon me. Middle-aged and tired though I was, I had come to glory.

10

MONEY FOR NOTHING. GUGGENHEIM AND OTHERS

The worst year in the lives of my friends was the year they got their Guggenheim Fellowships. They have not told me this, nor have they complained to Gordon Ray. For the envy of friends and the esteem of men in exalted places are prizes not lightly given away. But if you can catch one of your own lucky friends in an unguarded moment, ask him to tell you the truth for a change. The trouble is, though, that you have illusions, and the only way you are likely to get at the truth is by talking to a genuinely honest man. The conversation will go like this.

You: It must be a tremendous responsibility — even somewhat unpleasant — to be given eight thousand dollars to spend on research.

Guggy: All the kids had chicken pox in the fall, and we owed the doctor three hundred dollars. . . . Sailed for England with four thousand left. Then Gloria's parents came through with two thousand so we could spend a month in Greece.

You: That month in Greece must have been worrying, what with thinking you might get a telegram from Ray telling you to get back to work.

Guggy: Actually we were there only two weeks. Two weeks in Israel and

Syria, a month in Italy, a month in France, and a few days here and there in Yugoslavia and Spain.

You: But still and all you must have had the project weighing on your mind.

Guggy: Project? Oh, yes, I thought about the project.

You: And worrying about whether at the end you would have accomplished something worth eight thousand dollars.

Guggy: No, it's not like that. You couldn't pay Shakespeare eight thousand dollars to go write *King Lear*, and you can't give a scholar eight thousand and always expect tangible results. Ray probably thinks he's lucky if he gets two books for every hundred thousand dollars he forks out. It was no skin off my back that I came home without anything.

You: I suppose the real thing is that the experience is meant to broaden and deepen your thinking, and that's why your hair turned gray.

Guggy: God-damned bastards. I tell you I kissed the earth when we got back to God's country — student riots and all.

You: Well, yes, I don't suppose I'd care to eat grasshopper soup or whatever it is they eat in Syria. And someone was telling me how terrible the university system is in Italy.

Guggy: It's the god-damned English I'm talking about. We had to spend five months there, and it was like solitary confinement in a cold hell.

This conversation does not cover the experience of all my friends. I well remember the chief exception, who spent twelve of his twelve months in England, and on Tuesdays, Wednesdays, and Thursdays, when the British Museum is open from nine till nine, he was there from nine till nine. I was sitting in a pub nearby one summer evening, and he lurched into it like a gray substantial ghost — a hundred and seventy-five pounds of dead flesh. He got his Guggenheim so he could finish his book on a nineteenth-century author, a book he had been writing for ten years if not longer. The book was done except for some footnoting, and he spent his year doing that footnoting; and now six years later the book is still

69]

not published, not even finished for all I know. That man hated the English with a passion two and two-fifths times as great as that of his friends.

But we all want Guggenheims anyway, and two thousand dollars from the American Council of Learned Societies would be acceptable. So I will describe my successes and failures on the path to obtaining twelve thousand dollars for my own worthwhile projects. My first grant came in my first year at Brunch University, when a local man gave money to the English department to encourage research. The department itself decided to distribute the sum among a few junior members, a decision that I imagine was wholly altruistic, made in the belief that originality and need lay with untried instructors and assistant professors. I am inclined to think that such altruism usually operates in the giving of grants, so there is hope even for the most obscure young man with a worthless project. At the time, I despaired of getting any of the money. There were forty other junior members of the department, most of them with a year or more of service and some of them with terrifying abilities. I could hardly write my application. It came to a page, and surely it ought to be ten pages. But one morning the chairman of the department stopped by my class and told me I was among the lucky four. In memory that day is confused with the day the first Sputnik was launched. They came about the same time, and exhilarated me in the same way — new planets swimming into my ken. Ever since then I have applied for grants regularly and kept my applications short.

I sailed for England on that grant to find the drafts of McPherson's poems, and came back with nothing much to show for my thousand dollars, and they gave me another thousand the following summer for more of the same. Eventually I published an article in *JEGP* that was based on a draft of one of his romances that turned up at the New York Public Library, and I had a footnote in the article to thank the department at Brunch for funds that helped with the preliminary research. The article appeared a year after I was fired from Brunch, and the chairman knew he had wasted his money without seeing the article.

[70

It is a fact that the money that came hardest came where I had the most direct power. Just before I arrived at Baraboo University from Brunch, my articles and books began to burst forth like flowers in the spring, and presently I brought my new chairman the finest blossom of all, my contract with the illustrious press to edit McPherson's letters. Only one man in that English department had ever written a book — a small book issued by a vanity press. Only two or three had ever published articles. I was a prize, and the president at Baraboo thought I was a prize, but even with his help I had to fight hard for my grants. For the grantors would listen to the president, but they knew that presidents come and go, and they knew that he had other quarrels on his back. They had been in charge of grants for years. And my chairman himself, a tired dictator, had no intention of encouraging egotism in a junior member of the department. All this obstruction I thought disgraceful at the time, but today it fills me with admiration. There must be some hope for an educational system where a few men do not absolutely worship scholarship and prestige.

My Fulbright was another matter. Once when I was in graduate school I nearly applied for a Fulbright award, but after that I never gave it much thought. The idea of uprooting myself to go teach for a year in foreign parts had no appeal for me. And when a Fulbright friend wrote me from a country near England and said, "How would you like to come and take my place next year?" I was of two minds. It was only that I was now editing McPherson's letters and needed to be in England that made the proposal attractive. My friend was an established scholar some years my senior, and a man with connections social and political; and I saw that this was how things were done. I said yes. And then I received a shock. My friend had assumed I would say yes and given my name to the Fulbright authority in the country near England. In a few days I had a letter from the authority regretting that funds for the following year were already allocated, and there was no place for me. My friend had overreached himself. Then several days later came another letter from the authority telling me to ignore their previous letter. Would I please send in my credentials. My friend had not overreached himself. In due course my application was approved on the transatlantic side and approved by the Fulbright Commission in Washington. All I needed was the formal approval of the State Department, and that I never had. I don't know what went wrong. Perhaps word of my radical politics was indexed in their files. More likely some wholesome objective man decided against me. But I never quite trusted the power of my powerful friends again.

As for my Guggenheim Fellowship, I used to dream of winning one, and the dream always ended with my saying: Who are you that you deserve a Guggenheim? And for too many years I actually thought that people deserved Guggenheims, and I could not bear to answer myself. Then one day a letter came from a friend, and the letter said: "Would you like a Guggenheim?" Just like that. I had sent this friend a copy of my recently published critical study of McPherson, and told him about my new articles; and though this friend was not Gordon Ray himself, he was the nearest thing imaginable – an X Ray as it were. I knew nothing of this at the time. He did not positively promise me a Guggenheim, but he thought I must be deserving of one and had a good chance. It would have been indiscreet of him to promise it, since he did not actually sit on the Guggenheim board, and I read this fact between the lines and realized that I was close to a certainty. But I felt unsure. My critical study was at best a narrow piece of scholarship, and my articles were none too many, and I was almost forty years old. I wouldn't have awarded myself a Guggenheim, and I didn't get one that year.

This was before I signed my contract with the illustrious press to edit McPherson's letters. On the day I did that, I began to think of myself as a deserving man. For Gordon Ray was an editor of letters; Gordon Haight was an editor of letters; Dan Laurence was an editor of letters; and their burdens had been lightened by the Guggenheim millions. Yet it was commonly said that Guggenheims were an award for past achievements rather than future, and it seemed unlikely to me that I would get a Guggenheim until the first substantial volume of McPherson's letters was in the libraries. I applied each year, and each year I received a mimeographed letter telling me that they had two thousand applications and money for two hundred awards. That figure of two thousand was enticing, though. It covered all scholarly disciplines and creative arts, so far as I knew, and gave hope that I was a one-in-ten shot, and eventually they might yield to a sense of chance or feel tired that afternoon.

Then finally the first volume of the letters was published, and three months later I had my letter from the famous old scholar at the famous old university asking me if I would come and take over his courses next term. He and my Guggenheim friend were one and the same man, and he dilated upon the marvels of my editorial work and told me there could be no question about the Guggenheim this time. He had talked to X just last night — down for the weekend — and it was certain. I wasn't quite as confident as he was, even though I was a fully deserving man, and still it was a shock when I received the mimeographed letter a few months later — sitting in the famous old man's chair in his office, a scholar come to glory, but without enough power to make a Guggenheim a dead certainty.

The famous old scholar telephoned me the next evening. He was shocked too. He had gone up to the Guggenheim offices that day and asked them what they meant by ignoring his advice. He would never write them any more recommendations. And he let one or two of those people know that I was a better editor of letters than they would ever be. And who had been my other references? Oh, no, that was too bad! I should have told him I didn't have anyone else with a real name! He would have got me a couple.

The Guggenheim people gave him an explanation, or he gave me an explanation. They were no longer supporting editions of letters of twentieth-century authors. Was it true? One award that year went for the letters of a twentieth-century American author. It may have been a special case. In any event, having failed for five years to win a Guggenheim for McPherson's letters, I am now submitting a new project. It is a project that may come to nothing, and may make me hate the English;

but if there is any justice in the world, I should have my Guggenheim before anyone reads that I haven't.

Of course I have had other rewards. One day in the British Museum I came across a former colleague at Brunch who told me he was in England partly on a grant from the So-and-So Society. I had heard of this society, but its name was so far removed from English literature that I never gave them a second thought. And here was one of the most foolish men I have ever known, and he had money from them. I went straight home and wrote them a letter, and they sent me fifteen hundred dollars in a twinkling. Of the American Council of Learned Societies I will say only that they have helped me on four separate occasions. I have spent their money wisely and well, on microfilms and Xerox copies and a custom-tailored suit — for my previous suit was patched in a place unbecoming to an American scholar.

11

HOW I HID MY IGNORANCE BEHIND THE SEVEN VEILS

OF WISDOM, AND HOW IT'S MORE FUN

TO KNOW YOU'RE NAKED

Short of proving that Milton was a Frenchman from Savannah, Georgia, I think the American literary scholar can demonstrate anything he wants to. In the poor sciences there are only one or two truths to arrive at, depending upon which piece of machinery you use. But in literature anything is possible, and you have only to pick up the latest issue of *PMLA* to see a glittering array of the latest truths. In moments of modesty the American scholar will concede that much of what is written is misguided and incomplete. He is as ready as the next man to take a long historical view and admit that the truths of today may be the follies of tomorrow. But his heart isn't in it, for he knows that there is indeed Truth to be arrived at in literature just as surely as there is in science. It may be more slippery, more subtle, than anything the scientist dreams of, but it is There, and he has a sneaking suspicion that his own articles on Wordsworth have arrived There. Tell him his articles are unreadable to begin with and irrelevant at the end, and you will offend him. Tell him you don't believe in scientific truth and he will know you are mad.

Yet I myself did a lot of scholarship in the name of Truth, and it was all lies. Sometimes I thought it was Truth, and sometimes I was gleeful at what I was palming off on the learned world. The simplest way to do this sort of thing is to become omniscient. You take a poet like Robinson Jeffers, and it's surprising how few books and articles have been written on his poetry. In a matter of a month you can get through them, and at the very least you can sift the range of criticism and come up with an article entitled "The Critics and Robinson Jeffers." To get at the truth, you have to go a step further, and show how no one has said the right things about *Thurso's Landing*; and here you have infinite possibilities. The truth may be the sum of what each of the critics has imperfectly glimpsed; it may lie at the dead center of extreme views; or you may have to dive off a deep end yourself. The truth may be encapsulated in an image at the beginning of the poem. It may be hidden in the climate of the times. It may exist bald and naked in a first draft or in letters that Jeffers wrote to a horse. Be sure that if you sit in front of *Thurso's Landing* long enough you will see things that no one saw before. Not too many years ago my colleagues and I used to worry that Knowledge was increasing by such leaps and bounds that we would soon be out of work. No fear of that. The more that is done, the more that needs to be done. Who, for instance, will begin the task of clearing away the rubbish of the past two decades?

The first deliberate piece of deception I ever attempted came about inadvertently. I was trying to get at the heart of an inconsequential story I was teaching, and the heart seemed to lie in the fact that the hero had only one eye. A few years before, I had read an article by Freud on Polyphemus, and I went back to that article, and between it and my own reflections I came up with an original interpretation of the little story. I wrote an article on it, and wrote in all critical confidence except for the ending. My intention at the end was to play God or God's first lieutenant, and show that with Freud's analysis as a guide, one could uncover new truths about any and all works with one-eyed characters in them. But I had the misfortune to use for this conclusion one of the great stories of the world. The critics had been working on this great story for years,

[76

and had not got within a million miles of it. Now here I was with a blue-print from Freud, and I sat in front of the story with the blueprint beside me, and I thought and thought and thought. And nothing came. I tried for a hundred hours, and I remained a million miles away. Something was wrong. Could it be Freud or modern criticism? No, the fault lay with me, and all I could do was pretend there was no fault. I laid out the blueprint at the end of the article, and told the reader that if he followed directions he would get to the heart of the great story. I actually thought somebody could get there, and the man who published the article told me he did.

This failure worried me. At first I thought it reflected an abuse of insight on my part. One has to approach art with a diffident sort of attentiveness. Had I been teaching the great story instead of the inconsequential one, I might have had my truth about it, and then gone blind on the other one. Blueprints are for engineers, and intuition, humility, concentration, indirection, and responsiveness — all suspended across the wires of reason — are the lot of the literary scholar. Is not this a pleasing thought? I worked it up into a new truth, namely that critics and their criticisms, geniuses and their wisdoms, evolve and decline. There is the time in which they mature, there come the moments of inspiration, vision, and discovery, and there follows the declension into schemes and blueprints. This was not my own truth, but I thought of it for myself, and no sooner had I done so than I was invited by a friend to read a paper at a meeting of the Modern Language Association. Here was my subject, and I cast about for a famous literary critic and took two of his masterpieces of criticism and showed that the one written in 1925 was inspired and the one written in 1940 was mechanical. I buttressed the argument with material from his life and letters, for he was an unusually famous critic, and I surprised myself at how readily I was able to fit everything into place. Not that my method was lacking in science — for does not hypothesis precede proof? I was lucky, it seemed, in lighting upon a hypothesis that could not fail of proof. Yet before I finished that paper I began to think that it didn't matter whether the hypothesis could be proved or not.

Give me any old idea, I said to myself, and I can argue it from any old case. The exhilaration of this thought contributed greatly to whatever eloquence and persuasiveness the final draft of that paper had.

Since then it has been easier for me to write my articles. If you are worried sick with trying to get at the truth, chances are your flow of ideas, your style, and your sense of humor will suffer. Have you read every last word on your subject? Have you shown that you know the latest critical perspectives? Have you made your case airtight? All calculated to turn your article to stone. Not that my recent articles are light entertainment; for the rules and regulations of American scholarship remain too severe to permit the godless acts that scholars in England can perpetrate. But what I do now is write my article first and decorate it with learning afterward. Whether the result is more readable than the stone tablets of my colleagues I cannot say, but I enjoy the writing more. Freedom from truth gives energy to my imagination, and leaves energy for footnoting.

No doubt such an approach can be as complacent as the pursuit of truth, but I have a hard time believing so. Absolute and appalling smugness is the mark of the wise man, and you can see it shining through the most admirable modesty. Said the modest Socrates: "The unexamined life is not worth living" — thus killing at one stroke the people for whom the unexamined life is not worth leaving. How often I have been told that I cannot understand seventeenth-century poetry until I understand the seventeenth-century mind, and then I have been led through a maze by an immature twentieth-century mind, and come out starving to death. A friend of mine who has studied the seventeenth century for at least seventeen years swore to me that he had not yet cracked the meaning of Andrew Marvell's "The Unfortunate Lover"; and was I to believe he had failed to read Rosamund Tuve, Louis Martz, John Wallace, and all the other people who have cracked the seventeenth-century mind? — or was I to believe that he was hovering on the brink of new knowledge that would transform everyone else's knowledge into ignorance again? I might have told him what I thought — that a sensible high school boy could get the meaning of the poem the first time around — but that would have offended his modesty, and he would have become angry with me.

Not long after my friend told me this, I had a curious experience with a poem I had been reading for thirty years. One of my colleagues at Baraboo University became ill, and I took over her course in American literary theory, a subject about which I had hoped to remain ignorant. I handled the course by transforming it. We would study the early poetry of a particular American poet, and try to infer from it his poetic principles. Next we would go to his prose writings of the time, and see what he thought his poetic principles were. Then we would read his critics over the years and see what their poetic principles were and what they thought his were. Finally we would try to tie these things together in various ways, and we would repeat the process with a couple of other poets. I didn't know where we were going or what we would find out, but I kept a week ahead of the students, and the course was altogether pleasant. Came the day when I read this poem, a poem of fifty lines, and I enjoyed it as much as when I was in high school, no doubt in part because I had never taught it before. Then I read the poet's writings, and I lighted upon an odd phrase that seemed to describe the poem with special aptness. Then I read the critics, no one of whom had gone at the poem with this phrase. Instead they had gone at it with Christian symbolism, with the poet's weltschmerz, with the weltschmerz of the poet's times, and so on, and they had all gone absurdly wrong. I thereupon dashed off an article on the poem, and in the next months I went through all the poet's writings and all the critics — for I was using a small selection in the course — and documented my case. So far as *PMLA* was concerned, where the article was published, I demonstrated that only by a right understanding of the poet's theory could one arrive at a right understanding of his poem; but what I proved to myself was that I still understood the poem the way I had understood it in high school. The accumulating weight of my wisdom had somehow failed to bludgeon my perception of the poem to death. I was so pleased with this realization that I nearly fell into a new truth; namely, that the more learning is brought to bear on a poem, the less sense will be made of it — a truth to which my own experience was the noble exception. I have settled for it as a half-truth.

But I ask you — my colleagues — to call to mind those conversations you occasionally have with intimate friends in which you mutually confess ignorance of vast tracts of learning. You have never read *Middlemarch*, George Moore is no more than a name, *Finnegans Wake* might as well be a sacred book of the East. You are an Elizabethan scholar but you have never read the whole small body of Elizabethan plays. You teach world literature, but every foreign language is a mystery to you except French and German, and they are familiar terrors. For how many years have you dreaded someone saying, "Do you know that spot in *The Devil Is an Ass* where . . . ?" In fact you have survived hundreds of such moments by nodding a polite assent, as much as to say, "Yes of course, go on, I'm following you," but almost as much as to say, "No, I've never read the play, but don't let me interrupt you," in case he asks you a genuine question about it. Now as you confess your ignorance you laugh the uneasy laughter of scholars. A trace of self-satisfaction enters your voice, and you contemplate so-and-so who has read all the Elizabethan plays and knows Latin. A piece of decayed flesh he is, a trained ass. Do you not believe, in this moment of self-satisfaction, that a lot of learning is the devil's own instrument?

12

ACADEMIC FREEDOM, AND THE FIGHT BETWEEN
JOE MC CARTHY AND CASPER MILQUETOAST

There is a college in Massachusetts that used to ask prospective
teachers whether they smoked or not, and if they smoked, they were not
encouraged to teach. There is another college in Massachusetts whose
president asked me what my religion was when I went to his office for
an interview (but he was a former minister who owned shares in an
Egyptian oil company, and my prospective chairman apologized for his
behavior afterward and eventually he was removed from office). Academic
freedom is a frail plant, and we can all tell tales of times when the plant
was uncherished, unwatered. The tales are amusing and horrendous by
turn, and they illustrate our own dedication to the high principle; and if
we live in Massachusetts they prove that Massachusetts has one or two
courageous men in it.

The classic tale, of course, concerns Nazi Germany, and we know
how a great university system collapsed because of tyranny from without
and cowardice within. The tale that follows is a small affair by comparison, but I happen to be the hero of it. Furthermore, it has a new interpretation that is relevant to the new crisis of American universities, and

the new interpretation transforms me into one of the villains. The time is the early 1950s and I am teaching at a college in Massachusetts, and the shadow of Joe McCarthy lies across the land. He and his friends are exposing Communists in the government and the universities, and the Communists in both places are called before committees in Washington to admit their lies, confess the error of their ways, and name their fellow conspirators. Why the fear? According to certain colleagues on my right there is nothing for an honest man to fear, and the aim of the exercise is to purge universities (above all) of liars and cheats. For a Communist in America, even if he is not explicitly the servant of a foreign power, must blink the terrible facts of Communist history, distort the facts of American life, and be unworthy to bear the name of teacher, intellectual, and scholar. Other colleagues not so far to the right regard the situation more compassionately. To err is human, they say, and what man among us has ever been in possession of all the facts of a case, has always kept his emotions in rein in thinking his intellectual thoughts, has never rushed too hastily into a generalization? One or two eccentrics go further, and argue that many of the brilliant achievements of the human mind have been made in prejudice, error, and ignorance — whether it is Kepler devising simple movements of the planets because he knew God originally wanted it that way, or Einstein leaping to conclusions that were yet to be tested sixty years later. If all the liars and cheats are to be removed from the universities, these eccentric colleagues say, the universities will be emptied. Universities exist for clever liars and cheats to have the chance to succeed brilliantly. This is what academic freedom is about, and we don't need bigots coming in to upset the delicate operation. And then there are the colleagues on my left, and they are all quaking in their boots, for they know that the real issue is blood — their blood.

My own position is anomalous, for though I think I belong to the left, I am not quaking in my boots. I hear a sociology professor declare at a public lecture that he no longer feels free to discuss Karl Marx in his classes, for fear his students will carry tales. He holds no brief for Marx, he tells us candidly, but Marx is an important figure, and the university

[82

that ignores him is ignoring its intellectual duty. I blush for the man's false cowardice, false courage, false intellectuality — for I have uttered all manner of blasphemy in my classrooms and never heard a word of complaint from my superiors. A scientific colleague tells me that he is being followed by FBI agents who suspect he might decamp to Russia with his clever brain. He is a friend of mine, and I try to calm him down. A historical colleague tells a small private gathering that if Eisenhower wins the presidential election America will descend into fascism. A hysterical historian, surely! And then a philosophic colleague tells me I maintain my philosophic calm only because I am young and have no family to worry about if I am fired. What a curious way to think!

Why is it I am not quaking in my boots? Sad to say it is in part because I am an honest man. I have no talent for conspiracy, for party politicking, or even for joining. Out of social conscience I have forced myself into an uneasy alliance with the Democratic party, but my deepest inclination is to express my right ideas under my own banner. I am innocent of smoke-filled rooms of whatever color, and what could Joe McCarthy bring me to Washington for except to make a fool of himself? And therein lies the other reason I am unafraid. McCarthy is a man whom it is impossible to take seriously. He is scum, and I think the American people will find him out soon enough. The bogey of fascism is so insubstantial to me that I am half inclined to vote for Eisenhower. I have always liked this peaceable soldier, and Adlai Stevenson strikes me as an awkward uncomfortable man, whose speeches aren't nearly so elegant as my friends say they are.

Then comes the first crisis. The national office of the American Association of University Professors sends out a resolution affirming that no teacher should be dismissed from his post merely on the grounds of his being a Communist or on the grounds of his refusing to answer possibly incriminating questions put to him by the House Un-American Activities Committee. The resolution comes to the college chapters for their consideration. Now the chapter at my college is dominated by liberals and radicals, and the resolution is assured of easy passage. Yet people are nervous, and one hears that the case against the resolution is going to be argued by the new political science professor, a man reckoned to be as clever as he is conservative. Who will be able to stand up against him? One hears too that he is gathering about him some old and honored members of the chapter, and a quarrel could bring the chapter down in ruins — this fine chapter that has fought the good fight so often in the past. And lastly one hears that in a practical way there is nothing to quarrel about — there is only one supposed Communist on campus, and he is not a member of the teaching faculty. Why quarrel then? At this point I begin to be afraid, for I see that I who have nothing to lose, who have no friendships with old and honored members of the chapter, who have quite a clear notion of the rightness of the resolution — it is I who must lead the argument against the political science professor.

My fear originates in stage fright. I have yet to learn to be more than half at ease in my classrooms, and I have never said more than "aye" or "no" at meetings of the AAUP chapter. I will have to screw myself to my task. I do. I prepare my case. I bring John Stuart Mill and Justice Holmes up to date, and I inform myself minutely of the argument of the enemy. Two or three years later when the members of the Supreme Court get around to a decision on the issue, they use my logic. But I have to face the political science professor on my own, and now I am also beginning to succumb to the general alarm. Am I merely offering myself free to witch-hunters? Is it possible that I will be carted off to Washington and abused and embarrassed if not exposed? Are things come to such a pass that presently I will be denounced for the admittedly outrageous and inappropriate things I continue to say in my classrooms? Have I misread the temper of the times entirely? What chiefly saves me from this hysteria (apart from a natural inability to take life wholly seriously) is the certainty that I could never survive under fascism. If we are descending to that, I might as well get on with the battle.

Comes the meeting. It is not crowded, and familiar faces are missing, and I have no sense of an impending test for democracy. The tension in the air seems largely to be my own. One of the first persons to speak is my scientific friend. He is still being pursued by the FBI, and he blurts out in a single sentence his belief in the resolution. All of us shrug our shoulders. The political science professor speaks. He proves to be thick-headed, and he merely says that the day a person signs himself into the Communist party he signs himself into conspiracy and intellectual disgrace. We listen as though he is reporting on a garbage disposal plant, and that is what he thinks too. Does anyone else wish to speak? No one? I do not rise. I have too much to say, and I would prefer that my liberal and radical colleagues share the burden. But no one speaks. My scientific friend looks at me. Other people shuffle as though the meeting is about over. Then our lone supposed Communist rises. I do not know whether he is in fact a Communist, but he has been named in private conversations, and why shouldn't he be? I have seen him on campus before, and I have looked at him in the way one does, to see if the mark of communism is upon him. He is shy and lonely. He is soft-spoken and soft-mannered. He strikes me as being clumsy, ineffectual, stubborn. In short, a bad conspirator and a petty intellectual. Now he speaks, and do my colleagues look at him with bodies drawn back and faces averted or contemptuous, as though they are a German faculty and he the lone Jew? All these years later I imagine that there is just a whiff of this in the air; but mainly I have the sense that the man is regarded as an inconsequential outsider and no one has any intention of listening to him. He speaks of the American Revolution and the ideals of dissent and of everything else except the immediate issue. He sits down. Does anyone else wish to speak? I speak. My speech is there before me in the front part of my brain, laid out points one, two, three, and four. I start awkwardly and then it comes all right. But where is my audience? I know a half-dozen of the people here, and my words are not for them. I know a few others slightly, and the rest not at all. How do I talk to them? I catch faces looking at me curiously, blankly. Presently I am listening to the sound of my voice. The issue must have been settled last week in two smoke-filled rooms, where the conservatives agreed on what their spokesman would say and the liberals and radicals decided not to fight. I who thought I was going to sway multitudes by right-minded eloquence am talking into thin air. I plunge on with less and less conviction, abbreviate bits here and there, and come to the end with relief instead of a peroration. Does anyone have anything else to say? Someone calls for the question. The meeting has begun with a motion rejecting the resolution of the national office, and now the chairman asks for the vote. The ayes come from every quarter of the room. Noes? Silence. Then the lone supposed Communist says no. I am so filled with chagrin, confusion, and contempt that I say nothing.

But it is a famous victory for the liberals and radicals, I hear afterward; for the conservatives were content to defeat the resolution and did not press a counter-motion calling for automatic dismissal of Communists and pleaders of the Fifth Amendment. There was a courier between the two smoke-filled rooms.

The second crisis comes more than a year later. I have left the college but am still in town. The lone supposed Communist is named as a suspect in Washington. He is summarily dismissed from his college post by the president (the minister with Egyptian oil shares). I talk with friends on campus, and it is no affair of theirs. I search my soul and decide it is an affair of mine. I have now met the supposed Communist formally (I will call him Smith) and I telephone him and say if there is any way I can help, I will help. I become his raft in a storm that blows him out of sight.

A non-storm storm, except for him. Five or more years before, I learn, Smith had close friends among the liberals on campus, but they left him some while before the AAUP resolution, and none of them comes around now for old times' sake. He is competent and nonpolitical in his college duties, one of the old friends tells me, and the president has no right to fire him; but it is a bad case, and who wants to make things more difficult than they are — for anyone? (This old friend is the man who apologized to me for the president's behavior.) The campus is quiet. No one even beats his breast and says he is still afraid to teach Karl Marx. Everyone is waiting to hear whether Smith will clear his name in Washington.

Smith and I meet in his car — less incriminating for me, he thinks, than his or my house. Of course he is not a Communist, but Washington has no right to investigate him, and he will plead the Fifth Amendment. Foolish, I say; you must object to the proceedings, and say only what you think is honorable to say, and refuse to hide behind the Fifth Amendment. Self-immolating, he says — though he would like to tell Washington that their whole rotten system should be overthrown. Absurd, I say, for surely with all its ills capitalism is doing better than socialism or communism. Naive, he says, and revolution is just as right in the 1950s as it was in the 1770s. Nonsense, I say, and I turn red white and blue. Nevertheless our meeting gives him comfort, and we conclude that whatever he does he should not go to Washington without consulting a lawyer. In a few days we find one who is willing to talk to possible Communists, and we go have a conversation with him at twenty dollars an hour. In all of this I remain rather more calm than hysterical, and my chief sense of unease lies in the fact that Smith and I do not especially like each other. I have to pretend concern and trust where I feel none, and I wonder not so much whether it is a bad case as whether the only good case is where one acts as friend for friend.

The lawyer says: You are not a card-carrying Communist? and do you know what I mean when I say card-carrying Communist? Well and good. Now tell me about the sorts of political meetings you have gone to. Have you attended meetings where the announced speaker was a known Communist? where the occasion was sponsored by the Communist party? where there have been known Communists in attendance? Etc. etc. I falter in my attention for a moment, and then I hear him say: Have you ever attended meetings under security, with special identification for entrance, and armed guards? Shocking question; for the lawyer is clever and knowledgeable, and he cannot be asking the question unless such meetings of Communists in America do occur. A repellent image of conspiracy fills my mind. Can soft-spoken and ineffectual Smith have attended such meetings? I hardly know, even though he says no. Presently he and the lawyer go off to talk alone, and I am left wondering about my naiveté if not my honor. I do not regret I am there.

Some days later Smith and I take a train to Washington and I wait in a corridor while he and the lawyer plead the Fifth Amendment. Over the next few weeks he and I see each other socially, but we cannot be friends, and he is preoccupied with finding a new job in another town. Before he leaves he gives me a book from his library, a collection of Max Beerbohm cartoons. And that is the end of the affair, and I sit out the rest of the McCarthy era with nothing much to do. My political virtue is intact and my liberal thinking polished to a high degree, but I hope that I do not have to offer my services to other local suspects. I have dreams of going to Washington on my own, taking with me only my peroration and my contempt for both inquisitors and Fifth Amendment; but I realize that no one is going to give me the opportunity.

What a curious and unsatisfactory tale it is, and I cannot even dredge the usual moral from it. For of course I had to ask whether academic freedom suffered at the college, and the answer was no. Was there tyranny from without? Yes — though much less than was imagined. Was there cowardice within? Yes — and I will admit that I thought then that everyone I knew was a coward, and the only difference in my opinion today is that I will include myself. Why then didn't the walls fall down as in Germany? True enough the measure of a fall may be difficult. In Germany there were famous scholars seen to be leaving the country and various departments of universities seen to be closing up shop, and decades later there are no names of German universities to ring across the world as they once did. My Massachusetts college had no famous scholars, and not even an obscure one chose to leave, and no departments were shut down. One could judge the fall only by the odor of the place, and insofar as I could judge, the odor was the same before and afterward, and the pursuit of truth continued at the same pace.

Perhaps this proves that I saw the situation wrongly, and that discretion was the better part of valor, and my colleagues fought the good fight after all. But no, it wasn't like that. There were ironies in the sequel, too.

[88

By the late 1950s these same colleagues and others across the land were complaining of the new apathy among students. In our time as students, these colleagues said, we were glad to get to college, and knew what college was about, and we were inveterately political (even if sometimes wrongheaded — but what is youth for?); whereas students today want snap courses, fraternities, and soft jobs afterward. It was cause for public concern, and there was agreement that faculties must make a greater effort to challenge the minds of their students and show themselves as living examples of the free spirit. Much emphasis on the hard, energetic, and wild thirties; much ignoring of the early fifties! And irony still to follow; for by the middle 1960s who could deny that American faculties and students together had become the very example of free, inquiring, energetic men? Name almost any department of studies — mathematics or physics, architecture or fine arts, English literature or sociology — and the Americans were a beacon to the world.

Surely this proves that I was wrong about the early fifties or that we were all wrong. McCarthyism was a mere pinprick, a momentary upset in a body that was going from strength to strength. But no. All the facts stared me in the face, and I finally came to accept the cardinal one: that academic freedom and academic cowardice go hand in hand and nourish each other.

This is not to say that academic tyranny and academic cowardice do not go hand in hand as well, or to imply that I am no longer committed to a certain notion of academic freedom — I do not know what I would do without it. But I now think that truth is a lie and universities are places for liars and cheats to lie cleverly, and I believe that the free pursuit of truth encourages spinelessness as much as tyranny ever did. How many other activities can be as safe, complacent, and comfortable? Granted that large minds have pursued truth and died nobly for it (and I am glad they came before me); but it is rather more hazardous to be a soldier. Once you are within the fold of Catholic truth or scientific truth, you may be able to go on for centuries without fear. Or if you have fear, it will be the sort that bounces harmlessly off your armor as you lie and die. You are Casper Milquetoast himself, but you have coined new wisdom about Wordsworth or analyzed moon dust, and there is no one who can touch you, not even if you cringe before him. Why shouldn't such a man survive the early 1950s? Why shouldn't such a man have done well for himself since then? I have had shelter in his home, for which I am grateful, but I once argued his case for him, and I call our accounts square. My case now is that academic freedom matters in the respect of our trying to be civilized human beings — trying not very hard.

From such a vantage point I look at the classic German tragedy, and imagine how unpleasant the German academy must always have been. The cowardice of the thirties was implicit in the high dedication of the nineties, and the mediocrity of later decades is falsely measured. When Einstein, Planck, and other German scientists gathered in Berlin early in the century and congratulated themselves that no other nation could assemble so great a roster of scientists, they exhibited the ignobility of their calling and the blindness of German character to itself. Lucky the German academician of the second half of the century. He cannot indulge such complacency and arrogance, and he may help to civilize some of his countrymen.

Now today new irony is upon us, with the student revolution. Students became political again in the middle 1960s, and was it because we taught their elder brothers so well in the late 1950s? (Smile if you say that!) And some of us are becoming nervous, for we want to get on with the truth (faster and faster) and to say the least we are spending huge amounts of time persuading our students to get on with it too. Sometimes our persuaders are coffee and doughnuts, sometimes tear gas; but of course the real point is the freedom of the academy for unfettered intellects, and yes there are things wrong and intolerable and undemocratic, and we have sat on our hands, but the answer isn't to destroy the place. One of my liberal friends told me how some students at his university held a reactionary professor under siege for twenty-four hours, and it was only after a great faculty rumpus that my friend and others prevented drastic penalties from being imposed on the students. What finally was done? The students were given a research grant to investigate the influence of the reactionary professor's views — some such topic as that. My liberal friend laughed apologetically and said, "I know it's not a solution, but what would you do?" With another former colleague I got into a heated argument on the new crisis, and he finally said, "Do you mean that you think the whole university system should be destroyed?" I was trapped in my anger and said "Yes," and he blanched. "What can I say?" he went on. "I had a student say to me in my office not so long ago, 'What's the use of being literate?' How do you answer something like that?" Well what *is* the use of literacy if the cream of the cream proves to be clever and bold Casper Milquetoast? I see the exasperated student asking the question, and I have some hope for the student revolution. I also see poor old Smith. Was he genuinely exasperated too, and I so blinded by truth and conventional honor that I couldn't recognize it? It was civilized of him to give me the Beerbohm volume, and I cherish the volume now more than I did then.

13

ACADEMIC BRAVERY, AND HOW I AVOIDED
THE VIETNAM WAR

It is easier to be brave today than it was in the time of McCarthy, and many of us have long since stood up and been counted against the Vietnam war. We have signed away our names and a few dollars on newspaper petitions; discussed the war in books and articles, giving our royalties to hospitals north and south; refused to pay the portion of our income tax that goes to the war; marched and sung and spent a night in jail. The price for most of us has not been high, and we have felt the existential thrill and shared in the grand melodrama of American history. We may also have felt some real shame, too; for the Vietnamese have died faster than we, and surely have had fewer rewards in the way of self-advertisement or conscience.

I feel some shame in writing these words, for whatever the attitude I adopt, the emotion is academic, and whatever I feel is not enough. Neither I nor anyone I know has taken off his gown and gone to fight for the Vietcong, or tried to blow up the Pentagon, or even left the country because of the war — aside from going to Canada, which is hardly leaving. Collectively we might have brought the nation to its knees by 1967 if we had walked off our jobs; and why didn't we? The war has been an ideal war for us — loathsome as all wars ought to be, with both sides behaving reprehensibly in a way to flatter our sense of divine objectivity. As nationals of the one side, we have encouraged disengagement, and all too slowly acquired influence; and we have always been disengaged ourselves, if engagement is to be measured by the price one offers to pay.

I have heard about a man who did leave the country, but he was an Englishman to begin with. I have also heard much talk about leaving, but the talk has always ended on the note of there being no place to go — no place where the price is not too high. Could we leave Yale and its six million books and a salary of $19,000 to go to a provincial English university with fewer than six hundred thousand books and a salary of £3000? How could we advance Knowledge there? And could we afford central heating? We are rueful and moral, but we are also intellectual and comfortable, and America is the best place for us. So we make Thoreauvian gestures with our income tax, and perhaps have stabbing thoughts that our English department salary itself comes indirectly from military funds.

I myself began avoiding the Vietnam war before it started. In the middle 1950s I was publicity writer for the Democratic party in my college town in Massachusetts. I didn't like the job, I didn't like some of the men I wrote publicity for; I was doing what I could in an imperfect world. Luckily the man who headed the party was a decent person — I insisted on his decency even when I was told he was the puppet of a notorious reactionary Democrat in Washington. One of his patent acts of decency was to bring into the councils of the party a sociology professor at the college who had large-minded ideas about reforming the party and society, and for some while the two of them were to be seen planning the future. But presently the sociology professor decided that the sine qua non of reform was the removal of his friend from power, and because he lacked the capacity to do this on his own, he formed an alliance with a dissident party leader. Together they toppled their man, and then the dissident leader threw the sociology professor out and became both head of the party and mayor of the town. I was unaware of what was going on, but not surprised by the outcome, for the dissident leader had always seemed an unsavory character to me. For that matter, I had never been keen on the sociology professor. With the world more imperfect now than before, I resigned my post. I thought I had learned a few things: that a high-minded idealist can be as naive, dishonest, and harmful as the next man, that I ought to trust my personal feelings more, and that henceforth I should serve no cause except one in which I was wholeheartedly engaged. These reflections were supported by my experience of the McCarthy crisis in the same years, and the sociology professor was the same man who beat his breast over Karl Marx.

In the next several years I mainly kept aloof from politics of all sorts, and the times I didn't I seemed to learn the same lesson again. Of course my posture suited my temperament — I can hardly deny that; and it also suited my ambitions to get ahead professionally. But I did see little occasion for action. So the years of the Vietnam war crept upon me, and by the time the United States embarked upon paramilitary aid to South Vietnam I was at Baraboo University, where there was a peace group, opposed to nuclear armaments, generally opposed to war, and beginning to think about Vietnam. I attended a meeting or two of this group, and thought that the leaders were the same sort as my sociology professor. The group was not for me. Besides I wasn't a thoroughgoing pacifist or an unconditional nuclear disarmer. I could not know the ins and outs of foreign policy, and though I distrusted Kennedy more than most people did, I did not think he lacked conscience, and I was content to leave the keeping of the peace to him. Presently he showed the two sides of his character in the Bay of Pigs debacle and the Cuban missile crisis, and what could I have done about either affair? One of the leaders of the peace group told me in a heated argument that the whole missile episode was plotted out by Kennedy and Khrushchev together to serve their political careers, and I saw all the more reason to keep clear of the likes of him. By 1964 I was beginning to feel uneasy about my position, but in that year I happened to get a job abroad for several years, and it was in those succeeding years that the price that academics were willing to pay was mainly paid — paid by the peace group at Baraboo and elsewhere. I suppose I would have joined them again had I remained at home; but I cannot deny that my aloofness was facile and my concern tardy. In 1967 I did return home briefly and made a contribution. I taught an undergraduate course that had only boys in it, and I vowed at the outset that I would give no boy a grade less than 70 — I would not make him available for the draft. And on the last day of class I told everyone that I was going to be impertinent. I am a middle-aged man, I said, with nothing to lose, and have no business advising you; but I hope you have the guts to burn your draft cards. I said this with the bitterness, the helpless anger, the restrained self-righteousness, the visionary glow so true to the liberal conscience, and went back overseas again.

And that is all I have done about the war, except to continue thinking about it — especially thinking about academics thinking about it. In turn over several years many of us have asked the question of the moment: who broke the spirit and the letter of the Geneva accord? who escalated first? who violated the demilitarized zone most seriously? who lied about the Gulf of Tonkin? who de-escalated in name only? We have ascertained the facts on each occasion, and they have salved our conscience or published our sin or justified the muddle; and we have congratulated ourselves upon performing the historic task of the academy.

Then we have contemplated the larger truths to which the facts of the case are incidental. Recall those lost days when doubt was barely above the horizon, before we even began to say that American idealism was caught — this once — in a morass. America did want to protect South Vietnam from Communist terror (we said); was honestly trying to conduct a restrained defensive war; and was genuinely bent on reconstructing South Vietnam while defending her. Had ever war been waged so selflessly, so compassionately, by great or small power? The American soldier with a chocolate bar — naive and complacent though he might be, and ill-suited to inherit the role of international policeman — that American boy was there with good intentions. Now today we contemplate other truths. The war has been a military adventure, a place for the army to test new weapons, for the air force to regain a larger slice of the military budget, for G.I.'s with comic-book minds. It has been the spin-off from technological man, the fruit of clean inhuman thinking about napalm, defoliation, and new villages. It has been a power game of an industrial-military-legislative complex that has usurped the authority of a democratic community. No matter that our new truths contradict the old, or that the path between them is strewn with confusion. We are learning all the time, and in the present we are always right, and duly bland and bold and cautious.

Lastly I think of the still larger truths that some of us are ready to impale ourselves upon. What does Vietnam mean to the national life? Has it destroyed the American dream, or has it merely made us sadder and wiser men? Does it mean a return to isolationism? Has it brought an increase of violence on television? Could the money in fact have been spent otherwise? We desire nothing more than to answer the most important questions of life, and eventually we will go to North Vietnam itself and find out what the war meant there, and any North Vietnamese who wants to know the truth will have to read our books. Someone has to do the job, and why not a trained fool?

There is a famous American scholar who got trapped in the Vietnam war in a way that most of us did not. He and other brave academics went to Washington with the Kennedy administration to open the new frontier in 1960, and they went amid your and my applause for the belated coming to power of the intellectuals. (But now we talk about the industrial-military complex.) And wise though they were, or perhaps in the smugness and corruption of their wisdom, they made wrong decisions, and this famous scholar endorsed the villainy of the Bay of Pigs and the war in Vietnam. Today his name is anathema to some of us who have merely had to display the courage of our convictions. He reminds me of my sociology professor in Massachusetts, and makes me wonder whether I should think more compassionately of that man's trickery. We academics are damned if we do, and damned if we don't.

Well, these thoughts I have had are churlish, and give no credit to the decency and honor of many people, myself included. I admit it. What chiefly troubles me is that our sense of American virtue in getting out of the war is too much like our sense of American virtue in getting into it — but as I write these words I hear about the Pinkville massacre.

14

COLOR ME BLACK

In my time I have shared many of the right ideas of colleagues up and down the land. The particular time I recall now is the early 1960s, and I have just returned from a splendid summer of scholarship in London, where out of the corner of my eye I observed the meeting of black and white in Notting Hill, a scene of recent racial disturbance. I am entertaining a fellow member of the English department at Baraboo and his wife, who are liberals of the same deep vein as I, and I know that our mutual admiration for our liberal ideas is indistinguishable from our respect for our scholarly competence. All the colleagues we despise as scholars belong to the right wing and the dead center of politics and society. How can the truth be in them? How can we even grace them with the name of American scholar?

I tell my friend and his wife that what English people call a riot, Americans would regard as peace and quiet. Notting Hill has achieved the sort of integration we dream of. Black and white couples stroll the streets with their offspring and pass unremarked. No street is a ghetto or a no-man's-land, each has its black and white families up and down its length, and the life of the street is shared. Moreover although some of the streets are poor and perhaps come under the technical definition of slum, the sense of the place is vastly different from the irremediable squalor of certain streets of Harlem. There is community and pride, and everywhere you can see the scaffolding that means paint and restoration. Tears glisten in my eyes as I tell this tale of the brotherhood of man. There is virtue in me, and my friend and his wife see it, and I see the virtue in them too. We could go on till two A.M. this way, and think there is some hope for a world that has such people as ourselves in it. But then I say: "The trouble is, I believe in England for the English, and the thought of English civilization dissolving politely into international ersatz has no appeal for me."

This brings my friend and his wife up short. They haven't suspected such heresy of me. But the subject still allows for fine discussion of the relation of culture to nationalism, and the inevitable drift of Western civilization, and they can ascribe my view to momentary perversity — perhaps my summer has been too pleasant. And then I drop my second brick, and it breaks up the evening. "The trouble is," I say, "that I think the races have a fundamental antipathy to one another, and a difference of mentality, that will be wiped away only when the difference in color is wiped away, and I don't want that to happen." What is especially shocking to my friend and his wife is that I say this from a point of moral and intellectual superiority that they cannot pretend to. I have taught at a Negro college and lived in a Negro community, and they have not.

And now six years later the revolution has occurred. The notions that were once so laughable — that the Negroes should set up their own nation in Arkansas or somewhere, or all go off to Africa again — have become thinkable in one form or another; and the liberal whites, especially the Jews, have seen a chasm open up before them. The situation may be as temporary as it is deplorable; but who now possesses a bland confidence in interracial harmony and understanding? I had a letter recently from my friend, in which he described a regional meeting of the College English Association where he and other whites were the subject of contemptuous remarks by arrogant blacks. How times have changed!

he said. How he himself had changed! He now said black instead of Negro, and he was nonplussed and offended.

If it weren't so serious it would be funny. Think of all the right-minded men who have argued the case for the same-mindedness of male and female, and then got married and found their wives to be irrational animals from another planet. Think of the long, fervent, and unconvincing arguments that there is no such thing as Jewish mentality, or that German sons bear no taint of their fathers' crimes, or that there is no necessary connection between culture and nationalism, or that culture thrives best where there is social freedom, or that the English and American novel have become one. We can appreciate the generous impulse behind some of these views, but one and all they seem to me to reflect a scholarly aptitude for blindness, and it is no use saying the reverse views are just as blind. Still I shouldn't condemn my colleagues without condemning myself, and here is a true account of race relations in my own academic life.

See me on my very first day in kindergarten. I am in tears and I am afraid because seated next to me is a dark-skinned boy who looks like an animal from another planet. The crisis is brief and the boy proves to be southern European white; but this innocent stain upon my reputation is indelible, and forever afterward I am conscious of difference between myself and others, of whatever sort. All the same I was not the wicked little monster that children are sometimes reported to be, and during the rest of my years in public school I had a tendency to make friends with Negro children; for my cardinal virtue was sympathy with underdogs and outcasts, and I was not long out of kindergarten before I knew the views of some of my family and the white part of my hometown. One or two of my school heroes were muscular Negro boys, and I had a shy friendship with the one Negro boy in my class. But that was about all. When I went away to college I found a single dark-skinned boy among three thousand students at my famous university, and I assumed he was an Indian prince and thought no more about the matter. And then I went into the army and was thrown in with southern whites, and there began the baffling and absurd arguments that have continued

[100

to this day. I have broken up friendships and intensified enmities, and sometimes I think I have contributed nothing to the true cause of racial tolerance.

In any event I arrived at the year 1950 a convinced, vocal, and self-righteous liberal, and I was looking for a teaching job. Virtually none were to be had. Things were at such a pass that I went for an interview at a military prep school in spite of a ferocious loathing for things military. Luckily I was not offered that job, or my shame might have been greater than it was. For the only alternative post proved to be at a Negro college, and how could I have forgiven myself if I had been able to make the most cowardly of choices? As it was, I went south to my Negro job with shame enough. Not long ago a dean at Harvard transferred himself to a Negro college, and there was some self-congratulation in the white community for this useful act. But virtue comes easily if you wear the badge of success. I myself was a young man who lacked success and who wanted success badly, and going to a Negro college was the surest sign I was not getting it. My liberal principles enabled me to keep a stiff upper lip, but I could not hide my shame from myself. I was ashamed of my shame, but it would not go away. Could life be worse even if I were a Negro?

I was naive. I got on my first southern bus some few days after my arrival and sat with the whites. But what if a Negro colleague were at the back? Should I ignore him? Or wave to him distantly? And what if the bus got crowded and a Negro woman stood next to me, especially a Negro colleague? The next time I rode the bus I stood all the way, and stood at the invisible dividing line between black and white. Thereafter I sat with Negroes, and there sometimes followed a little scene in which the bus driver stopped the bus and told me I couldn't sit where I was sitting, and I got off the bus. I realized I wasn't made for public demonstrations and violence, and these scenes were hateful to me, but I knew whose side I was on, and in later years I always forgave myself for the quiet pride with which I related my experience.

The college itself practiced segregation of a subtle kind, in which the

Negro majority discriminated against the whites and among themselves, and the whites did likewise against the Negroes and among themselves. It was fascinating, and worthy of a sociologist's nice distinctions, but I caught mere glimmerings of it before I left, and my experience was chiefly with a young group of Negroes and whites who practiced color blindness. Within this group I had a more agreeable social life than I have had before or since at white colleges, and I flatter myself that one or two of my Negro friends said to themselves that I was a decent human being and not like every other white person they knew. But the chief thing I realized about my group was that none of us were color-blind and none of us were going to be after twenty years' practice. With my most intimate Negro friend there was scarcely a moment that I did not think his was a black skull and mine a white and that our worlds were different. We had fine and easy times together, and yet at some point or other our conversations touched on race and became troubled; and I knew for a certainty that he lived in a constant rage against white society. I myself had experienced something faintly like his rage in my two years of service in the army, but here it was consuming a man's life, and if I understood it, I remained outside it, a white man to myself and to him, a friendly enemy.

My reflections did not please me, and I had others that embarrassed me, and yet I could not keep them down. My Negro colleagues discussed *Beowulf*, recited more stanzas of *The Faerie Queene* by heart than I knew the first lines of, and professed to love Thackeray. Wasn't it odd and incongruous? Didn't they have any shame in surrendering to the enemy culture? Shouldn't they be teaching Swahili? These thoughts were so entangled with other unworthy thoughts that they surely had to be nonsense. Who was I myself to be teaching *Beowulf*? The thing was a muddle.

Even in deliberate abstract thought I led myself astray. In this and earlier years I read a good deal about race — about the unlikelihood of multiple origins of mankind, about the physical characteristics that make the white man more like an ape than the black man is, about rising intelligence quotients of Negroes who move north and go to white schools, about Negro geniuses, about mixed harmonious societies. In some corner of my mind these truths all seemed like lies, and the one important fact seemed to be color. If Henry Adams could ascribe the violence of the American character to the violence of the American climate, why should not one think that color of skin had a profound bearing upon one's being — quite irrespective of learned social attitudes? Once I began to countenance this heretical thought, the hostility between black and white seemed as natural and inevitable as that between male and female.

Presently I was fired from the Negro college, and I returned north with some relief to write the first of my dissertations, and in the next eighteen years I sorted out the confusion. The process had more to do with new experience of white society than black, for my friendships with former Negro colleagues faded, and my contacts with Negroes were reduced almost wholly to the conventional meetings that a liberally minded white teacher will arrange. See me now at the end of the road. I am teaching at a famous old white university, and it is summertime, and one of the great residential halls has been turned over to Negro youths in a program called "Upward Bound." I talk with a white boy who is helping to run the program, and he tells me it is giving a chance to kids who never had a chance. What sort of chance? I ask him, and I see in my mind's eye a famous white scholar at another famous university who recently gave a series of public lectures on Jonathan Swift. Ask any knowledgeable person to name the half-dozen great authorities on the eighteenth century, and surely this man is one of them, and I see him spelling out his right thinking to his meek white audience. He has analyzed Jonathan Swift's wit, but he has never in his life uttered more than a wisecrack on his own, and his morose face seldom breaks into even that broadest of expressions. In his provinciality he is the very essence of international scholarly ersatz. He looks like an elephant dancing. What sort of chance then for Negroes? The ludicrous intelligence quotient of white America? The expertise of dullards? The complacency of hollow men? Black men into imitation white ersatz? Strange conclusion to Negro history. I have been at this famous old white university for six months now, and the two most interesting, most human beings I have met here and elsewhere during this time are the Negro short-order cook at a diner where I ate breakfast for a while and a Negro boy who gave me street directions. They aren't like whites, and I don't want them to have white hopes of becoming American scholars and engineers and vice-chairmen of General Motors and poets and astronauts and presidents of the United States. I suggest something of this sort to the white boy, and he smiles sheepishly.

I know what I do want, but doubtless it is impertinent enough of me to tell fellow white Americans what I think, let alone black ones, and I will leave it at this. One morning recently I picked up my daily paper and saw a picture of an armed Negro student shaking hands with the dean of students of Orlon University. At the point of a gun he had cowed a white administration and a white faculty into concessions and perhaps into imagining something was wrong. I don't like guns, and I didn't like Orlon, and the more things change, the more they can remain the same. I wouldn't say the picture was one of hope. But in my heart I was pleased, and you will flatter me if you say my heart was black.

15

OF COURSE I HAVE A SOLUTION, AND IT WON'T WORK

The trouble is, there's nothing to solve. Let me show one of the smaller ways in which the scholarly life is better than before. It used to be that scholars prepared concordances by hand, and it was the labor of half the lifetime of several fools to do such jobs. But this loss and wastage was necessary, for concordances were valuable, and you merely hoped that the work was indeed done by fools instead of by wise men. Time passed, and concordances became more valuable, for Caroline Spurgeon began to talk about word clusters and image clusters, and she must have gone blind sorting those things out. And time passed again, and some clever young American scholars went to talk with the people at IBM and learned how to extract concordances from computers after merely sixty hours of programming – divine concordances, as a matter of fact, for to err is human. In so doing, these clever young men became famous scholars overnight with their names on thick computer books. And the *Times Literary Supplement* sneered at them and asked if this was scholarship, and the clever young men asked in turn whether it was not better that machines performed such labor and that scholars spent their precious time on exalted thoughts. I myself read these exchanges, and

I liked the reasoning of the clever young men, but it also happened that I knew one of them, and he looked like a computer to me.

There are dozens of ways to prove that the whole educational system in America is getting better all the time, in spite of student unrest, and you have only to pick up your alumni magazine to see why. There you will be told about the new research library, the more rigorous entrance requirements, the open-ended seminars, the dormitories designed to bring faculty and students together, the visiting scholars and chamber orchestras, the higher class averages — you name it, it's getting better, like American society itself until suddenly we have decaying cities, riots, and the Vietnam war on our hands. Not long before his death that serious man William Clyde DeVane summed up twenty-five years as dean at Yale University, and to him it was an unblemished advance in every respect named and a few others, so that anyone would have thought that Plato's Republic was at hand on several square blocks in New Haven. Even when American educators incline toward modesty they cannot help thinking about the poverty of English dons, the fantastic promotion procedure in Italy, the infuriating rigidity of the whole system in France. Of course American education has its defects, always will have, but it's merely the best in the world and draws scholars from Europe as fast as flies are drawn to garbage. Think of the achievements of American textual criticism, think of the great biography of Joyce, think of the most learned man in Christendom (who teaches at Johns Hopkins, a friend told me). Can they be sneered at? And then think that the University of Texas has accumulated half the manuscripts of the civilized world, and will soon have more than there are altogether.

I have nothing to say to this. It's all true and false. What I know is my experience, recorded with unexceptionable honesty in the past several chapters, and my experience says that American higher education is a low-grade farce. Never mind the rest of the world. And I think many other scholars say the same thing when they contemplate their own lives, the lives of the colleagues they know, the character of the university they teach at. The trouble is we suffer from American idealism, which is another word for American naiveté. We trace the paths of students A, B, and C over their four years at college and are appalled or depressed by what happens to them, but we are also proud of the fact that more and more young people are coming to college every year, and we believe that education is the solution for all ills. We can count the bitter and dreary years of our own lives, but we help to push through the new Ph.D. program at our small college, and we are impressed with the fact that five times as many Ph.D.'s are awarded today as were awarded thirty years ago. We know that nine-tenths of our colleagues cannot read five lines of Shakespeare with half the expression of an English schoolboy, and yet it is fine to think of all those folios and quartos at the Folger Library. We dream of leaving our dreadful university, and never imagine that Swarthmore, Claremont, and Harvard are just as dreadful. What help is there for such people?

Any thought about improving American education has to reckon with the fact that the ivory tower is one of the central edifices of American society, not isolated and lonely and splendidly superior, but as American as mass production and bad food in a clever package. Any genuine improvement will have to come with a genuine change in the character of American society. There are all too many changes that are fake to begin with. Think of the grandiose gimmicks that Harvard announces every twenty or thirty years and that are meant to take the country by storm, and sometimes do. Think of the wonderful independent gestures made by Chicago, Johns Hopkins, and Yale during this century. All of them are more apple pie. They reflect and encourage the American delusion that civilized and occasionally great men can be engineered into being if you only know the right tricks — and of course one of the tricks may be to seem to look the other way.

A few years ago Radcliffe announced a grand scheme to salvage the talents and skills of women lost to domesticity. You and I have seen these women — bright girls who almost took their Ph.D.'s in biology and then found themselves pregnant. They spent the next eight years washing diapers and then at thirty-four or thirty-nine when the children were out of the way, the best they could do was to get a job as routine laboratory assistant. They were bitter, and some of them were bitter from the time they were pregnant. Radcliffe would keep tabs on these women, it would search them out, and it would invite them back to Radcliffe at thirty-four to take refresher courses, take degrees, and be fulfilled. Now here I think was an improvement specially designed to make things worse than before, and I knew it wouldn't work the moment I read of it in the *New York Times*. For though American women are as discontented as American men, it is not part of their American dream to believe that fulfillment in middle age comes with a degree and with dreary professionalism in a male prison. So far as I know, Radcliffe has retrained three biologists in the intervening years, and American womanhood is not much worse off than before.

Inevitably my own solution to the mess of American education falls into either of the two traps. It must be a gimmick, like the Harvard programs, or un-American madness, like the Radcliffe. Let me merely mention how I would face the problem that Radcliffe wants to solve. I would try to discourage women from going to college at all, particularly to Radcliffe. It's not the woman scientist or the woman philosopher who is civilized but some girl who reads Jane Austen, likes witty conversation and real flowers, and loves her children. Not impossible if she goes to college, but not helped if she goes to college. I met a Radcliffe girl recently, and she was filled up to here with the psychological-sociological-educational nonsense that is invented especially for the female mind; but she was a sweet warmhearted girl in spite of it all, and I wept to think of such superb resistance to evil.

Much of my solution comes to this: less education instead of more; less education in the interest of more civilization. What America needs is less knowledge, fewer facts, less professionalism, less skill, less efficiency, less progress. Will we get them? Not on your life. Look around yourself and see the dozen ways in which any one of our virtues is helping to kill civilization. But we all subscribe to *Life* as well, and there the dreadful machine of American culture glitters in several colors. It will grind on inexorably. Still I must offer my solution, not to the whole educational mess, but to the literary scholar's life. It is part gimmick, part madness; and for every respect in which it fails, please remember that I have thrown my book at the scholarly life, and that is really the best I can do.

Graduate School. Residence requirement for the Ph.D. will be satisfied in two years full time, residence to imply only that the student is living near the university and can use its facilities if he wants. For commuting and part-time students residence will depend upon a calculation of available free time. All lectures will be public lectures, with no attendance required or recommended and with no papers, examinations, or grades; subjects of lectures will be announced week by week. Students will have no program of work except (1) to consult occasionally with an adviser, (2) to prepare two papers, one of about fifty pages due at the end of the first year and the other of about one hundred pages due at the end of the second or later, and (3) to take a single examination, at the end of the second year or later. The second of the two papers will constitute the dissertation. In no case will it be allowed to be more than one hundred and twenty-five pages, and whenever the candidate is twenty-four years old or older the faculty may at their discretion waive the writing or the completion of the paper. The examination will consist of (1) a general examination on English literature and (2) an examination on a single century of the student's choosing. Every student will be allowed to try to pass the examination four times.

A list of readings will be provided the student at the beginning of graduate study. It will be a minimum list, not a maximum one, and the student will be expected to master it. The emphasis will be at least nine-tenths upon literature, and one-tenth or less upon scholarship and criticism. The latter will be restricted to a few exemplary books and articles. The character of the examination will be announced a month or more in advance.

For any student who wishes it, there will be a program of practice teaching in the undergraduate school. No credit will be given, and no notice of it will be taken on the student's records.

A master's degree will be available to those who want it after a full year of such study and satisfactory completion of the fifty-page paper at the end of the year.

Hiring and Promotion. No one under the age of twenty-four will be hired for college teaching, and no one who lacks his residence requirements for the Ph.D. Anyone who is hired will assume he is a permanent member of the staff, barring insanity, wickedness, or his own desire to move on. The competition of ten instructors for three slots as assistant professors will cease. Any university that finds itself saddled with too many clever young men who turn out to be fools need consider itself no more unlucky than the best universities today. Promotion will be automatic and will normally depend upon age. Everyone should be a full professor at forty.

Teaching. Oscar Wilde's apothegm will be the guiding principle: "Education is an admirable thing, but it is well to remember from time to time that nothing that is worth knowing can be taught." Any teacher who imagines himself to be either a fountainhead or a cargo plane of civilization will be asked to think again. New instructors will be warned against correcting much more than mechanical errors on freshman themes. All classes will be dismissed as soon as the teacher feels inclined. Each teacher will be left to his own devices.

Research and Scholarly Publication. The basic attitude toward these will be that an evening in the garden or an evening reading Keats's poems in an armchair is more likely to keep civilization within reach than an evening poring over Keats's manuscripts at Harvard. But there is no reason why a man should not do all three, and even if a man insists on doing only the last, it will be permitted. He will be advised that he must find his reward in the work itself. The university will not encourage him. The university library will be chary of buying scholarly books, and it will buy no manuscripts except those that pertain to its own history and the history of the local province.

Textbook Writing. This will be prohibited unless the would-be author can persuade his own department and a committee from another university that his book will not duplicate a book already on the market and that it has sufficient merit to warrant the waste of his time.

No, it won't work. It's like my thinking years ago that all the Shakespeare folios and quartos at the Folger Library ought to be given back to the English. I survived that. I decided America deserved to have them. We deserve everything we get. We will continue to study those folios and quartos, long and seriously, and in time we will become deadheads absolutely and incurably; and the poor English will be left with Shakespeare himself, to misunderstand, ignore, and enjoy.